Chaos Marketing

Also available in the McGraw-Hill Marketing for Professionals Series:

COMPETITIVE RETAIL MARKETING:
Dynamic Strategies for Winning and Keeping Customers
Andrew Collins   ISBN 0 07 707567 6

MANAGING IDEAS FOR PROFIT:
The Creative Gap
Simon Majaro   ISBN 0 07 707598 6

VALUE-ADDED MARKETING:
Marketing Management for Superior Results
Torsten H. Nilson   ISBN 0 07 707655 9

CUSTOMER-FOCUSED MARKETING:
Actions for Delivering Greater Internal and External Customer Satisfaction
Ian Chaston   ISBN 0 07 707698 2

MARKETING AUDIT CHECKLISTS:
A Guide to Effective Marketing Resource Realization
Aubrey Wilson   ISBN 0 07 707760 1

STRATEGIC MARKETING:
A European Approach
Jean-Jacques Lambin   ISBN 0 07 707795 4

BRANDING IN ACTION:
Cases and Strategies For Profitable Brand Management
Graham Hankinson and Philippa Cowking   ISBN 0 07 707757 1

TARGETING FOR SUCCESS:
A Guide to New Techniques for Measurement and Analysis in Database and
Direct Marketing
John Ozimek   ISBN 0 07 707766 0

INTEGRATED MARKETING:
Making Marketing Work in Industrial and Business-to-Business Companies
Richard N. Skinner   ISBN 0 07 707768 7

QUALITY ASSURANCE IN MARKETING:
Setting Action Standards For Better Results
Keith Sparling   ISBN 0 07 707876 4

FORENSIC MARKETING
Optimizing Results from Marketing Communication—The Essential Guide
Gavin Barrett   ISBN 0 07 707900 0

Details of these and other titles in the series are available from:
The Product Manager, Professional Books, McGraw-Hill Book Company Europe,
Shoppenhangers Road, Maidenhead, Berkshire SL6 2QL
Telephone 01628 23432 FAX 01628 770224

Chaos Marketing

How to win in a turbulent world

Torsten H. Nilson

McGraw-Hill Book Company

London · New York · St Louis · San Francisco · Auckland
Bogotá · Caracas · Lisbon · Madrid · Mexico
Milan · Montreal · New Delhi · Panama · Paris · San Juan
São Paulo · Singapore · Sydney · Tokyo · Toronto

Published by
McGRAW-HILL Book Company Europe
Shoppenhangers Road, Maidenhead, Berkshire, SL6 2QL, England
Telephone: 01628 23432
Fax: 01628 770224

British Library Cataloguing in Publication Data
Nilson, Torsten H.
  Chaos Marketing: How to Win in a
  Turbulent World. – (McGraw-Hill
  Marketing for Professionals Series)
  I. Title   II. Series
  658.8

  ISBN 0-07-707991-4

Library of Congress Cataloging-in-Publication Data
Nilson, Torsten H.,
    Chaos marketing: how to win in a turbulent world / Torsten H.
Nilson.
      p.   cm. – (McGraw-Hill marketing for professionals series)
    ISBN 0-07-707991-4 (pbk.)
    1. Marketing – Management.   2. Sales promotion.   3. Chaotic
behavior in systems.   I. Series.
HF5415.13.N538   1995
658.8–dc20   95-1442
                                                                  CIP

12345 BL 98765

Typeset by BookEns Ltd, Royston, Herts
and printed and bound by Biddles Ltd, Guildford, Surrey.

To my parents Enoc and Maria Nilson
—they never let chaos enter our home!

Contents

THE MARKETING SOCIETY

The Marketing Society is the professional UK body for senior practising marketing people. It was founded in 1959 and currently has 2300 members.

The aim of the Society is to provide a forum for senior marketers through which the exchange of experience and opinion will advance marketing as the core of successful business growth. To this end it mounts a large and varied programme of events, and provides an increasing range of member services.

Series foreword

The series title *Marketing for Professionals* was not chosen lightly, and it carries with it certain responsibilities for publisher, authors and series advisers alike.

First, the books must actually be intended and written for marketing practitioners. Most, if not all, will undoubtedly serve a valuable purpose for students of marketing, but from the outset the primary objective of this series has been to help the professional hands-on marketer to do his or her job that important bit better.

This commitment in turn has helped to establish some basic ground rules: no Janet-and-John first steps for toddlers, no lessons in egg-sucking for grandmothers (who these days may have a Business Studies degree), and equally no withdrawal into the more esoteric and abstruse realms of academe.

It follows that the subject matter of the books must be practical and of topical value to marketers operating—indeed, battling—in today's rapidly evolving and violently competitive business environment. Cases and case material must be relevant and valid for today, and where authors deal with familiar marketing tools and techniques it must be in terms which again update and adapt them, bringing them as close as possible to what in the current idiom we call the leading edge.

This has set demanding standards but, to the calibre of authors contributing to the series, perfectly acceptable ones. The authors are either senior marketers or else leading consultants and marketing academics with a strong practical background in management. Indeed a number in both categories (and as the series extends it is to be hoped a growing proportion) are themselves members of The Marketing Society, with the prerequisite level of seniority and experience that that implies.

McGraw-Hill, as professional in their field as the target marketers are in theirs, have consulted The Marketing Society extensively in the search for suitable topics and authors, and in the evaluation and if necessary revision of proposals and manuscripts for new additions to the series.

The result is a well-presented and growing library of modern, thoughtful and extremely useful handbooks covering eventually all aspects of marketing. It is a library which every marketing professional will want to have on his or her bookshelf. It is also a series with which The Marketing Society is very pleased to be associated, and is equally happy to endorse.

Gordon Medcalf
Director General
The Marketing Society

Preface

The most important conclusion from my work with marketing in a changing and turbulent world is that change is 'good for you'. The more one looks at the change processes and how a company can use, manipulate and make money from change the more apparent it becomes that change is on the side of the alert business executive. This said, change also exposes the company to risks, such as challenges from competitors and customers.

My main objective with the book is to give guidance on how a company can operate successfully in a changing world, to make more money by understanding and manipulating change.

The theories, concepts and relationships I introduce in the book all have their origins in real life experience. In my view the only proper way of building a framework is to look at the real world and draw conclusions, and conceptualize from my own experience or that of others. Some of my conclusions will probably seem fairly predictable but hopefully I shall have spread some new perspective on the issues. Other conclusions will be more surprising, explaining and illustrating new perspectives on marketing. Both aspects are important and in the spirit of 'chaos' it is impossible to determine beforehand which will be the most interesting.

Two disclaimers: please note that I have, as a rule, used the word 'product' in the book in a generic sense but the reasoning is applicable to services as well as products. There is also in the book a bias towards consumer goods in the examples and references. The reason is not that I consider one type of marketing more relevant than another, but the best conclusions come from one's own experience which, in my case, happens to be consumer goods marketing. I do believe, however, that the concepts are as relevant to industrial as they are to consumer goods.

I would also like to add that if I have been over-zealous in explaining professional expressions, please accept by apologies; if terminology has been left unexplained, I have done so to avoid boring those familiar with the jargon.

I have enjoyed writing the book, and I hope that you and your company will prosper with the help of *Chaos Marketing*.

Torsten H. Nilson
Oxted, Surrey, 1995

Acknowledgements

I would like to thank everyone who has made this book possible.

I am extremely grateful to all my colleagues and clients who, over the years—knowingly or unknowingly—have contributed with views and ideas that I have used in formulating and explaining chaos marketing.

I would also like to mention the inspiration I have had from the following books: *Managing Chaos* (Kogan Page, London, 1992) by Ralph Stacey, *Chaos Making a New Science* (Sphere Books, London, 1988) by James Gleick and *Foundations of Corporate Success* (OUP, Oxford, 1993) by John Kay. Most of the 'scientific' background has its origins in the first two of these titles.

In addition to my own experience, I have used several different sources for my examples, in particular *The Economist, Financial Times, Harvard Business Review, The Wall Street Journal*, the Swedish *Veckans Affärer*, the UK trade journals *Marketing, Marketing Week, Campaign, Marketing Business, The Marketing Society Review, Supermarketing, The Grocer* and *Checkout*. The data in the Levi's example in Chapter 2 is mainly from *Advertising Works 7*, the 'volume of record' of the seventh IPA Advertising Effectiveness Awards.

Of course much credit has to go to my wife, Annika, and our children for tolerating the many hours I spent in front of the word processor instead of resolving the chaos in our garage by rebuilding it.

I would also like to mention the assistance I have had from Mrs Irene Morton in handling the finer points of the English language.

Finally, I am grateful for inspiring comments from Mr Gordon Medcalf of the Marketing Society and the support from everyone at McGraw-Hill.

PART ONE

MARKETING AND THE CHANGING WORLD

1
Introducing change

Change is the only constant. We have always lived in a changing world and over the last decades this has become more pronounced than ever. Information technology (IT), changing social contexts and even political turmoil have influenced and will influence the way we run our businesses.

Marketing needs to be in the forefront of this change process. Marketing executives need to understand how to win in the turbulent world we are facing, otherwise our companies will cease to exist.

I shall not bore the reader by presenting long lists of how the environment and society around us are changing. It is, nevertheless, essential to understand that there is a never-ending process of change, that this process moves at different speeds in different business environments and that there is a difference between real and perceived change.

The process of change never stops. The economists' view that there is an equilibrium where supply and demand meet and that this is the only lasting level is only theoretically correct. Looking at the world around us it is quite obvious that even if an equilibrium could be reached it would not remain for very long: either the supply or the demand function would change due to human ingenuity.

Past theory has assumed that the ideal and ultimate situation is one in which all factors are in equilibrium, and that is the situation we should strive towards. As I shall show later in the book, this is (a) a goal that cannot be achieved for the medium/long term (at least within a 'free' economy) and (b) not even desirable, neither for the business community nor for the general public. The main reason is that without change there would be no progress and without progress we would not improve our standard of living and, as business people, would be left without a role.

It is important to realize, however, that the speed of change varies in different sectors of the marketplace. Over the last decades we have seen dramatic changes in the area of information technology—adversely affecting companies such as IBM.

In other market sectors we have seen a gradual deceleration in the change pattern. Today, for instance, it takes significantly longer to introduce a new product in the retail trade than it did 25 years ago. While IT has made it possible to obtain immediate information on what is actually happening in the stores, it has, with the 'help' of many other changes, also made it more difficult to get the products into the shops. If we go back to the time when manufacturers supplied goods direct to the local owner-managed shop, products could be introduced on the basis of one call and delivery took place the same day. Today, buying committees take the decisions, based on careful evaluation by the buying staff who have been briefed by sales managers who in turn have been briefed by marketing executives—a process that normally takes months.

Turbulence can be created relatively easily within environments that are perceived as fairly stable. For instance, if one of several retail competitors decides to take an initiative such as a drastic price cut, then, given the information flow and the mobility of the consumers, the other competitors will have to respond quickly. Turbulence is created.

EXAMPLE 1.1

In November 1993 Tesco implemented a cut-price promotional policy in frozen ready meals in response to similar activities from so-called discounters. For instance, Tesco cut the selling price for a pack of Lasagna from 99p to 59p. That decision had been planned for many months but, once implemented, that single decision changed the trading environment. The main competitor had to respond, and the following week J Sainsbury's had a similar product on offer at a similar price. In total a great number of packs were sold with subsequent brand share changes. In a business sector where, for several years, quality had been more important than price, one decision regarding one promotional price changed the competitive situation and a reasonably stable environment was thrown into turbulence.

EXAMPLE 1.2

This example from the car industry illustrates the reverse situation. Today it requires a skilled and knowledgeable observer to distinguish between year models. A 1992 model Ford Scorpio is very similar to a 1993 model. In the 1950s, especially in the USA, a distinctly new model was created every year; factories were closed down for retooling and the dealers and customers treated each year's model as a totally new product. The speed of change in this respect has slowed down.

These two non-IT examples illustrate that change is everywhere but the speed of change differs not only from industry to industry but from activity to activity. At one stage one part of the business might be driving change, at another stage it may be other parts.

In order to be successful in a changing environment it is also essential to differentiate between a change that is really happening and a perceived change we are only observing. The way microtechnology has changed the information flow and created new business sectors is without doubt real change, but in many instances we only perceive the world to be changing more quickly than it used to.

The following quote was heard on television in December 1993: 'The music scene changes every six months nowadays, you have to keep up!' No, the quote was not from a recent 'Top of the Pops', nor was it from the Punk age or the swinging 60s, but it came from the mouth of Elvis Presley in the movie 'Jailhouse Rock', released in 1958!

It is claimed that, statistically, the average age of a commercial enterprise is 40 years; that in itself assumes some change, although the statistics hide the changes within the workplace and the way we work. At the same time it is worth remembering that the average age of the top 20 grocery brands in the UK is 56 years (according to a survey by A.C. Nielsen, published in *Checkout* magazine).

If you, as a company or marketer, understand change and how to manage within a turbulent environment you will have a competitive advantage and this book will explain how you can exploit that. If you do not understand or misunderstand change, you and your business will suffer and disappear from the scene.

Change management is as relevant to a fast-changing environment such as computer games as it is to a relatively stable environment such as the wine industry. One can even argue that it is more important to understand change if the environment is fairly stable: in such an environment that type of knowledge is a much rarer commodity and thus becomes a stronger competitive advantage than in the turbulent world of computers where only those who master the art will survive even in the short term.

At the core of this is the simple conclusion that change is only destructive if you do not understand it, and it is only a danger to the business if you do not have a framework to deal with it.

EXAMPLE 1.3

The media debate is not necessarily a good indicator of the changes that really are happening in society. In the late 1980s several books were published criticizing the society at large for pushing women into role models and spending more and more on cosmetics and similar products.

A survey published by the Henley Centre showed that the change taking place in society had nothing to do with women, but with men. From 1986 to 1989 the average time spent on personal hygiene by women did not change to any significant degree, staying at slightly over 10 hours per week. Over the same time period the amount of time men spent changed from around 8.5 hours in 1986 to 9.2 hours in 1989.

By understanding how the markets and the environment really change you can move one step ahead of those who just learn to live in a changing environment. By manipulating the elements that lead to change, disrupting a 'stable' environment or reinforcing change in a particular direction, you can gain further competitive advantage and you can exploit the opportunities that a dynamic market offers.

Marketing, change and chaos

Of the many departments comprising a company, it is more important that the marketing function understands change. If you do not understand how the marketplace is changing (or not changing), how competition is changing, how society is changing, etc., you as a marketing executive will not be able to fulfil the marketing role in a satisfactory way.

But to understand is only the beginning. To make an impact you have to understand how to manage in such an environment. In my search for a framework to use in this context I came across *chaos theory*. The fascinating aspect of chaos theory is that in a number of ways it provides us with inspiration and useful models to understand both the business world at large and how the marketing function can become more effective.

At this stage I would like to make it totally clear that my objective with this book is *not* to apply a scientific chaos theory to marketing; nor do I claim to have total belief in all the aspects of the chaos theory concept. What I have done is to use some of the chaos theory framework as an inspiration to be able to understand and exploit the turbulent future we are facing.

I have used the term *chaos marketing* to describe the activities and principles that should guide effective marketing in a turbulent world. While chaos marketing describes how many marketers feel regarding their working environment, chaos theory is, in my view, a slightly misleading expression. Chaos theory is not chaotic, it is a conceptual framework to describe how the world around us reacts to change, whether the systems are stable, unpredictable within boundaries or uncontrollable.

For quite some time it has been obvious that the traditional marketing concepts, as described in textbooks by Professor Kotler *et al.*, do not give sufficient guidance for effective marketing in today's and tomorrow's competitive marketplace. It has become apparent by evaluating successful, and not so successful, products, brands and companies that the chaos concept provides guidance on how one can design a useful and beneficial chaos *marketing* framework (Figure 1.1).

What then is chaos theory? A more detailed explanation is given later in the book but at this stage a short introduction is appropriate.

Chaos theory grew out of observing the reality, just as my concept of chaos marketing has grown out of observing the business world around us. Scientists, primarily working with weather forecasting, developed the concept from working with mathematical models to perfect weather forecasting.

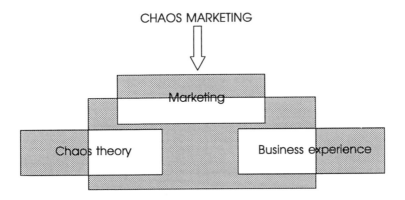

Figure 1.1 Designing a chaos marketing framework

During the 1950s and 1960s scientists were looking for ways of building the perfect weather-forecasting model. As we know today, they failed. In that failure lies one of the seeds to chaos theory. The elaborate mathematical models that were built, despite their complexity, failed to provide an exact forecast.

There were many reasons for the failure, such as the world is just too complex to be put into equations in a computer and any observation of the present, which is the foundation for any forecast, is full of approximations. The scientists also came to realize that the earth's climate will never settle into an equilibrium but provided there are no major interruptions in or to the system it will be possible to determine approximately what will happen. The scientific observations led to a conclusion that there is a repetitiveness in the system in the medium term but it is impossible to make exact predictions regarding what will happen next.

The weather forecasts with which the chaos scientists were battling are no different from the marketing executives' interpretations of market research data or the extrapolations of sales forecasts on the basis of a test market. The end result, real sales, will never be totally consistent with the research results.

As someone said, forecasting is difficult, especially when you are dealing with the future. In reality, on the basis of past experience it is only possible to have an educated guess at what will happen. It is also only possible to give an interval as to what is likely to happen. Anyone claiming to be able to do a detailed forecast is either lying or is extremely fortunate.

Also, due to the instability of the marketing world, some action will have a dramatic effect well outside the limits of its 'objective' power, while other major initiatives will go largely unnoticed. We have all heard the announcements of major technological breakthroughs (remember, for instance, the rotating cylinder engine used by NSU, once hailed as a major innovation?) with no reasonable short- or medium-term commercial results. On the other hand, there are many examples of a minor adjustment to a specific product creating great success, or a chance meeting setting off a chain of events leading to major commercial effects.

Summary

The realization that the world is not perfect, and never will be, gives important indications as to how to manage the marketing mix.

Flexibility, feedback systems, information interpretation, routines to deal with change (a useful anachronism in itself), interpreting the reactions to marketing actions, etc., are all factors that take on a different and important meaning in a changing business scenario.

2

Effective marketing

The more chaotic the world is, the more important it becomes to have a well-founded view of what one should be doing, and marketing is no exception. In the middle of a storm it is important to ensure that one is on the right track as a mistake can be very difficult to rectify.

This chapter will only cover the main points; aspects of most of these will be further elaborated upon in other chapters of the book.

The answer to the question of what one should be doing depends, of course, on the final objectives. Accountants have over the years debated the best criteria for success. I shall not fuel that debate other than to conclude that in the medium and long term it is essential that an operation generates a profit, as otherwise it will not only cease to exist (unless it is subsidized by someone) but it will also have no *raison d'être* as in a loss-making operation the component parts are more effective separately than as a whole.

To keep matters simple, one can conclude that the overriding criterion is to show a long-term profit. This has been formulated more elegantly and correctly by Professor Kay in his book *Foundations of Corporate Success* as 'the key measure of corporate success is added value. Added value is the difference between the value of a firm's output and the cost of the firm's inputs.'

In this context it is worth noting the difference between cause and effect. The long-term profit, or added value, is an effect of an efficient operation and similarly a high brand share is the effect of being competitive in the marketplace. A brand share figure in itself is not worth anything; it is only an indication of the level of superiority in respect of the competition and in the eyes of the market. Sustainable high brand shares only come from superior perceived value for money.

Moving from the generally applicable to the marketing sphere the role of marketing becomes: 'to constantly improve the perceived relative *value for money of the company's products or services'.*

As the most essential activity to ensure success is to add as much value as possible, the marketing department's overriding objective becomes one of *maximizing* the products' or services' tangible or material and intangible or abstract values.

It is, however, impossible to achieve relative advantages if one does not know the criteria by which the potential customer will measure the product or service.

The first step in effective marketing is to understand the total environment: the marketplace, the competition, the customers, the trends, etc. This is very basic but in a turbulent world it is more important than ever to have systems in place to monitor the behaviour of customers. It is also essential to have a good total understanding to be able to differentiate between real and what is only perceived change.

The international marketplace

One aspect that has taken on greater importance in recent years is the more international marketplace. Although many industries remain surprisingly national, the international element is becoming increasingly important. This is not only because more products flow across borders, but there is an increasing cross-national flow of information which moves much faster than in the past. The same trade magazines are read across the Western world; many countries share the same TV channels and the local publishers scan the world for stories to copy. At the more hi-tech end of the market we have the fusion of computers and telecommunications which has already started to affect all companies.

We see this in a practical way where, increasingly, the same advertising message, or an adaptation of the same message, is used across the Western world—or at least across most of Europe. This apparent *simplification* of the communication process is, however, rather the reverse. Using an international message effectively requires *greater* skills, as you not only need to create a message that has universal appeal but you must also adapt it to the local circumstances. At the initial stages of internationalization, many companies, especially some in the US, viewed the Western world as one market—with, in most instances, disappointing results.

An effective approach is based on identical core values but

adaptations to the local marketplace, combining the macro-approach with a sensitivity to the micro-environment.

EXAMPLE 2.1

Levi's used the technique of global strategy and national tactics over the period 1985–92 with great effect, modifying and adapting the now famous advertising within a framework and as a result achieving enhanced brand position.

Using the same basic building blocks the commercials and messages were balanced to suit each country. For instance in the northern European countries the tougher, more rebellious heroes were more aspirational, whereas in Italy, a softer personality was required. In addition, the various executions were rotated in a different pattern to optimize the effect.

According to Levi Strauss the mix worked in all major European countries with sales increases ahead of market growth by around 15 per cent in Germany, 25 per cent in the UK and over 80 per cent in Italy.

By focusing on a universal value dimension—freedom—and setting this value in a universally accepted imagery—'retro and Hollywood America'—combining it with an established imagery of mythical USA and adding a local 'tone', Levi's managed to achieve outstanding results in a very fickle and dynamic market sector—youth clothing.

Different market sectors have adapted a European approach to different degrees. In 1992 almost 25 per cent of all pan-European advertising was for cars: Renault, Fiat, Peugeot-Talbot and Ford were all on the list of the top Euro-advertisers. The second largest sector was toiletries and cosmetics, led by the French L'Oreal, with 14 per cent.

It is as easy to underestimate as to overestimate the rate of change to internationalism. In a 1993 comparison of the top 10 grocery brands in Germany, France, Italy and the UK only one brand featured in all countries, and that was the ever-present Coca-Cola. With a reduced criteria of being on the list in three countries only one more brand qualified: Procter & Gamble's Ariel detergent.

The pattern appears to be that a local brand will be more likely to pick up and exploit a trend than a relatively unknown international company.

EXAMPLE 2.2

In 1985–86 Ross-Young's, the second largest UK frozen food company, launched a range of prepared meals called 'Stir Fry' that was an immediate success. A few years later a German company, Frosta, launched a similar range in Germany, also with great success. And in

Sweden the local Findus company launched a Swedish adaptation of the same idea, again with excellent results. The same idea had been exploited by three different companies in three different countries. Information flow and an international awareness gave impetus to change. The companies close to the market exploited the opportunity.

Putting these aspects together it is clear that to be effective you have to be aware of what is going on around you. Change is fuelled by information and the information flow is quicker and more comprehensive than ever before—and the trend is towards even quicker flows in the future. Some of this change is real, some of it is hype and to be able to differentiate between the two is of obvious importance. It is also apparent that it is easier to exploit new trends if you have local knowledge and market presence. It is essential to understand the marketplace—not only the business realities but also the minds, the history and the culture of the recipients of the messages.

Optimize and maximize

To optimize the value maximization the skilled marketer must consider all aspects of the product (or service) mix. The intangible as well as the tangible product aspects must be enhanced. Without a sound quality base no company will survive, and to ensure success the tangible dimensions of a product must be superior to what is otherwise available.

To be able to judge whether a product or service is superior or not is a skill in itself. Mr Michael Cannon, at the time of selling his 550 chain of public houses to rival Greenalls, expressed it as: 'You have to be better than the next pub, but you don't have to be much better to succeed.'

Value for money has always been the final arbiter when deciding to buy or not to buy.

EXAMPLE 2.3

Andrex toilet tissue is an interesting example of value management in a distinctly unglamorous product sector. Andrex is a product with sound properties that has been supported by, and acquired, intangible value dimension(s) to ensure a strong brand position. Andrex (or Scott paper, the owner of the brand) has also been careful to ensure that the value-for-money perception has never been allowed to get out of hand.

The UK is one of the few countries in which toilet tissue is not a commodity. Despite a very heavy own-label presence in the UK grocery trade—for instance, for kitchen paper towels the own-label share is over 55 per cent—Andrex has kept or even improved its brand share. The total market has also benefited. Premium products account for over 70 per cent of the value of the UK toilet tissue market and the per capita value consumption is higher than in any other European country—for instance, double that of Germany, according to A.C. Nielsen, the market research company.

The reasons are a high-quality product, constantly updated and improved, and a strong brand personality built around a golden Labrador puppy.

The puppy was first introduced in 1972 and has, since then, played the main part in the advertising, illustrating the key elements of the brand properties, softness and strength, and of course adding the charm of a little dog.

In 1993, according to A.C. Nielsen, sales were around £180 million and in the yearly ranking in Checkout magazine of top UK brands, Andrex is No. 5 with a brand share that is well ahead of the competition at around 30 per cent.

Being better is not only about offering something better, it is also about being perceived as better, more interesting, more relevant. In a world with faster transfer of knowledge, building brand strengths (intangible benefits) is almost as important as ensuring product superiority in itself.

The key to success is to combine the tangible advantages with relevant and unique intangible benefits, as for instance Coca-Cola, BMW and Apple Macintosh have shown over the last decade.

While this might be seen as stating the obvious, judging from the marketplace, most companies have a long way to go. The current and future environment is not making it easier. To survive and prosper marketers need to adapt and change the working pattern. I shall explain how to use the changing marketplace to advantage later in the book.

Effective marketing: a few general guidelines

For any marketing operation to be effective it needs to be

- proactive, not reactive
- fast, not slow
- built on knowledge
- focused on a few key determinators
- offering the customer a 'better deal'.

To lead a market you need to be proactive. The successful
innovators do not *react* to events in the marketplace, they *create* the
event. Sony Walkman would never have come to the marketplace
on the basis of consumer research. The TetraPak company would
never have seen the light of day if consumer research had been the
arbitrator.

Using the knowledge of the market, however accumulated, to the
advantage of the business is to ensure proactive marketing. Leo
Burnett, the famous advertising man, expressed it as: 'If people
could tell you in advance what they want, there would never have
been a wheel, a lever, much less an automobile, an airplane or a
television.' The reactive principles of the marketing textbooks,
'fulfilling consumer needs and wants', was perhaps a key to success
in the 1950s and 1960s but in today's marketplace there are too
many companies who can supply what the customers want. The
reactive following of customer requests is just not good enough. To
avoid any misunderstandings, this does not mean that you should
not worry about the customer, rather the reverse, by being
proactive you can ensure that you *over-satisfy* your customers, even
surprising them with the quality of the offer.

The importance of rapid change in this context is quite obvious:
over-elaborate analyses become less and less relevant as, by the
time they are done, the world has changed again.

For a company to keep its place in a competitive market
environment, it needs to be as fast as possible as information and
communication flows more rapidly and in many instances the
innovations are coming onto the market more quickly than before.

However, speed is not an excuse for not being thorough—another
contradiction in today's marketing world, but a contradiction that is
manageable. During the 1980s much of the Japanese success was
built around being fast and using teamwork to combine
thoroughness with speed.

If you have to make and implement decisions quickly you need to
work from a solid base of knowledge, otherwise the decisions will
be less than optimal and the implementation will run into problems.
No filing system in the world can match what is in the heads of
experienced and successful managers. It takes time to build up
knowledge, and marketers often fail in this respect. Inconsistencies,
strategic mistakes and short-termism often have their roots in the
'intermittent' work pattern, i.e. the fact that they stay only a
relatively short period in one job position.

If you think, feel and believe that everything around you is changing you will need to know the background and the history as knowledge of only the present is not a reliable guide to the past. The reason for having to know the past is that there is one thing that is *not* changing, and that, in most cases, is the behaviour of customers. If the customers are normal consumers they usually live for 70–80 years and are potential customers for around 50–60 years. If the customers are companies the average age of a company is claimed to be around 40 years, again a substantial time period. It is self-evident that to be successful you need to have the same or higher level of knowledge of your products and your markets as your customers. Turbulence does not change that.

With more information flowing around the companies distractions can multiply as it becomes more important to stress the relevance of concentrating on the main, real issues. In terms of marketing that means allocating the, usually scarce, resources to those activities where the effect is best.

In most instances a purchase decision is based on a limited number of value dimensions. According to US research, around four or five value dimensions determine a purchase; in some cases just one or two. To achieve value superiority and over-satisfying the customers, the marketer needs to ensure that the product or service out-performs the competition in these key determinators. Especially in larger corporations there is a lot of waste in that too much time is spent on minor issues and not enough effort is put into ensuring that the product really performs on the key dimensions—those that will ensure long-term success.

Summary

Regardless of whether the market is in a state of turbulence, chaos or total stability, the customers must be ensured of the best deal. The customer is, of course, always the 'King' (or 'Queen') and the only way to ensure prosperity is to make certain that the customer each time is over-satisfied, i.e. the expectations are not only fulfilled but he or she feels that no one else could have supplied the goods in a better way.

PART TWO
CHAOS THEORY AND CHAOS MARKETING

3

A marketer's guide to chaos theory

The purpose of this chapter is to introduce concepts that can be useful in a marketing and business context. Just as it is easier to understand why a customer reacts in a certain way if you know the background, I hope it will also be easier to understand the concepts I shall introduce later to cope with chaos marketing if there is an understanding of where some of these ideas originate (Figure 3.1).

As mentioned in the first chapter, I do not intend to give a full account of the, in itself, exciting concept of chaos theory. What will follow is a selection of ideas that fit into the marketing world and are concepts that can help our understanding of what we should be doing to become more effective.

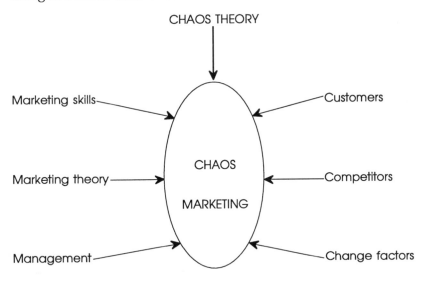

Figure 3.1 The components of chaos marketing

The three systems

In the past virtually all scientific models assumed that the optimal situation was a stable system and that stability was the ultimate 'version' of a system. Economics and other social sciences have also traditionally adapted this way of thinking. The theory was, and in many cases still is, that the various activities in a specific environment all converge so that, in the end, an equilibrium will be achieved. Most of the scientific literature has followed this reasoning although, in reality, there are very few examples of a truly stable system.

At the other end of the spectrum (Figure 3.2) we have the uncontrollable system or situation. In such a system all variables behave in a totally unpredictable way and we do not know what will happen in the next phase. In layman's terms a nuclear explosion is uncontrollable. Such systems tend not only to be impossible to control but also to be self-destructive.

In a sense, the old story about the straw that broke the back of the camel is an illustration of chaos dynamics—how a small additional amount of change can lead to a dramatic and unpredictable outcome.

In reality the most common form of system or situation is what the scientists now call a 'chaos' system. In such a system there is an unpredictability within boundaries. The system tends to react in an apparently random way without exceeding certain barriers. In several different areas scientists have discovered that systems work in an unpredictable way, showing all kinds of highly complex behaviour, but because of some inbuilt constraints in the totality the end effect is within boundaries, there is a non-repetitive repetitiveness.

STABLE SYSTEMS	DYNAMIC, CHAOS, SYSTEMS	TOTALLY TURBULENT SYSTEMS
(predictable, no change)	(change within boundaries)	(out of control)

Figure 3.2 The three systems

The dynamic 'chaos' system

The chaos system is by definition dynamic as we do not know exactly the outcome of whatever input we produce and the feedback loops that all systems have give effects that are not always predictable. The important and positive effect of this is that we get progression. The constant feedback from changes in the system allows everything to move forward.

We see this in our lives all the time. For instance, the effect of a drug on a disease is unique to each individual and each occasion. What has worked on one occasion might not work exactly the same way on the next.

This theory was first was discovered in weather forecasting. Until the 1980s vast investments were made in sophisticated computer models to predict the weather. At that time a modern computer would use 500 000 equations to try to predict the weather, with base information from every part of the globe. Despite this, as we know, the forecasts were not and are still not accurate. Beyond two or three days the world's best forecasts are speculative and beyond six or seven days more or less useless. The reason lies in the collection of the data and the arithmetic of making a forecast.

No data collection is perfect and, perhaps, when predicting weather that becomes more apparent. You cannot measure all parts of the globe all the time. And all those small microscopic deviations build up so that, in due course or in a matter of days, the differences have added so much to the predictability that the forecast is much less accurate than we would like to think.

This example illustrates two aspects of chaos theory. One is the total unpredictability of a real-life system. The weather happens to be a quite dramatic and changeable example of this and one to which we also all are exposed. The other is called the butterfly effect, as it is possible that the effect of a butterfly flapping its wings can change the local weather somewhere and that such a small local change, together with other changes, can influence the force and direction of the wind in some other area.

But although the weather is virtually unpredictable in detail, we can all give a reasonable prediction of what the weather will be next June in London. It is, for instance, most unlikely that we shall have snow and frost or a 45°C heatwave. Looking at past history we can estimate that it is probable that the temperature will be somewhere around 20°C but whether London will be bathed in sunshine or wet with rain we shall not know. Not even the meteorologists will be able to tell us that with 100 per cent certainty, even the day before.

The main reason for the weather to stay within the boundaries we have learned to expect, while not settling into a totally predictable behaviour, is due to the non-linear feedback systems. Effectively it is a complex feedback system, or loop, that is controlling a chaos system. One can also call the chaos system one with constrained instability, a combination of irregularity and disorder with boundaries and familiarity.

In the business world most of our ideas, thinking and planning of activities are based on the assumption that we are dealing with a stable system. We admire the companies that appear to have got everything right and those who produce the best results. The understanding is that these companies and their managers have managed to do everything right and as such deserve all our admiration.

They probably *do* deserve our admiration, but not necessarily for the reasons generally put forward. The successful operations have managed to perform in a way that has produced excellent results, but if we were to replicate what they have been doing it is unlikely that we would get the same results because at least some of the parameters will be different.

What we should admire is the way they have managed within the parameters of their business, and learn not from what they have been doing but from why and how they have been doing it.

At the other end of the scale—the uncontrollable system—we do not have a business equivalent, or at least nothing to admire. An uncontrollable business system ends up in bankruptcy or is taken over by the authorities.

The butterfly effect mentioned above has a very important business application. It illustrates that by giving a system a nudge you can trigger change. We have all in our personal backgrounds examples of how one simple action, usually one over which we had no influence, can set in motion a whole chain of events.

Many activities are unplanned and have unforeseen effects. What we can learn is that change can be set in motion by small events and that we cannot foresee what will actually happen. In economics we have a similar conceptual model in the so-called multiplier effect— that is, in a macro-economic context a small activity, such as the marginal tax decrease implemented by Nigel Lawson during the Thatcher years, can set in motion economic activity that far outstrips the initial change. One effect multiplies by another, and so on.

Of the three different types of system the chaos system is the one that most accurately resembles a business system and it is the one to use as a reference. It is not only the model that most accurately resembles the reality, it is also the one with the most favourable characteristics. The dynamics of the system generate adaptation to changing demands and generate activities that will move the company and the society at large forward.

The virtues of a stable environment is totally overstated. A stable system does not have the necessary inbuilt 'skills' in adaptation and it does not take into account the non-linear feedback loops that exist in the commercial world. It is also totally undynamic and as such is not only inappropriate from a commercial point of view, but it would make work very boring!

This leads to the conclusion that there will be no equilibrium anywhere. All assumptions will only be approximations and irrespective of how long we keep going we shall, for example, not improve our forecasting once we have picked up the basics.

EXAMPLE 3.1

One can compare this with the way trees and bushes grow in a nursery. If the gardener has some experience he or she will know what is required to enable a tree to grow. You need to ensure that there is water and fertilizers. On the basis of past experience the gardener will be able to predict approximately what will happen. Regardless of how carefully the gardener monitors the weather, the soil, the nutrients and the water he or she will never be able to predict exactly the size or shape of the tree. The gardener will only know approximately what will happen, and occasionally will be totally wrong.

The gardener will be considered a fool if he or she promises customers that trees and bushes, not yet grown, can be delivered to an exact shape.

In conclusion, all surviving business systems are to a degree chaos systems; otherwise they would not have been able to survive.

Systems and interaction

Chaos theory is built on a systems approach. It is the effects of the system which generate the various circumstances, not a singular activity.

Traditionally systems have two types of feedback loop, positive and negative. With our history of looking for the illusive equilibrium, negative feedback systems have usually created the most theoretical and practical interest. A typical negative feedback system is represented by the control mechanism for a heating system. At the beginning the system generates heat. After a while the desired temperature is reached and the negative feedback goes into action and cuts off the boiler. The next stage occurs when the temperature is too low and the feedback reacts to start the boiler up again. All these activities are aimed at creating an ultimate, even temperature, controlling the system to ensure that it does not deviate from the desired behaviour (i.e. a pleasant room temperature).

A positive system enhances any change. To continue the central heating example, a positive feedback would mean that when the desired temperature was reached, even more heating would be generated. The end result would be that the system would spin out of control and explode—become uncontrollable.

In business terms the negative systems are often used in terms of control mechanisms such as budgets. If a department deviates from the budget, the manager in charge is expected to react to ensure that the expenses or revenues will be in line with the budget in the future.

The positive feedback system in business is not used as often as the negative, but when pushing efficiency in an operation it can have interesting effects. It is also an essential part of personnel management, i.e. with positive encouragement, staff respond positively and produce even better results.

Different types of feedback loops exist in all businesses and can be used by managers who are aware of the various opportunities. The most important aspect of this—which is more fundamental and is often forgotten in case studies, descriptions of successful operations and market studies—is that everything, all actions, happen within a system and generate a response.

As we have seen, to predict this response in detail is often difficult or even impossible but, with the help of experience, in most cases it is possible to make an assessment of the boundaries within which the reaction will take place.

Each business decision and business action is part of a system. Most of the actions taken in any business are in response to something or someone. These responses are feedback loops in that particular system and will generate new responses, and so on. These systems exist between companies, between companies and individual consumers and internally in companies. All the systems and the response mechanisms that they trigger are of fundamental importance to our understanding of the workings of the dynamics of the business world.

Forecasting

As mentioned earlier, weather forecasting, and the lack of success within that discipline, was where chaos theory was first developed. Forecasting is also an area in which it is easy to understand the necessity for a changed perspective.

It is also fair to say that in many instances common sense has pre-empted chaos theory. In most large corporations long-term forecasting went out of fashion during the 1970s as the oil crisis in 1973 clearly showed that numerical planning was nothing but a piece of paper with some numbers. Nevertheless, forecasting and projections still take up a fair amount of interest and time, so the subject requires some elaboration.

The conclusion from the 'chaos' studies in the 1960s and 1970s was that any sequential forecasting model is flawed as long as it builds on the previous period, and that period's figure is based on a forecast (which is the most common situation in forecasting over longer periods, such as the weather forecast, the temperature in a house, the number of flies in a forest or the gross national product of a country).

EXAMPLE 3.2

Assume that the sales of a product reach 100 in January one year. The estimate is that this product will maintain a steady sales pattern across the year, i.e. no growth and no decline. This is of course unlikely to happen, so let us assume that the forecast is wrong by 5 per cent each month. If that forecast is wrong downwards in all the 12 months, the sales in December will be 57, almost half of the forecasted level. On the other hand, if the forecast is wrong upwards the December level will be 171.

Each of these extremes is unlikely to happen but this illustrates the impact of just a small deviation if it is repeated.

Assuming that the original approach is correct, i.e. that the sales development is more or less static, the likely development is that the sales each month will fluctuate up and down within certain boundaries, such as ± 10 per cent. We have a regular irregularity.

Linear and non-linear relationships

Traditionally all our reasonings have been based on linear relationships. If we add 2 to 5 we expect to get 7, just as we expect to get 9 if we add 2 to 7. While this logic is true for the simple linear relationships in the previous sentence, one of the key discoveries of the scientists behind chaos theory was that very few relationships are linear.

Scientists have always preferred linear relationships as a linear equation is easy to solve and it can be captured as a straight line on a graph.

Non-linear systems, on the other hand, cannot generally be solved, cannot be added together and cannot easily be described as a graph. We can pinpoint the relationship on a graph as we experience or observe it, but we cannot predict the behaviour as we do not know how it will behave when the parameter(s) change.

While linear relationships are easy to understand, are useful to explain relationships and in many cases serve as reasonable approximations, non-linear relationships are by far the most common.

EXAMPLE 3.3

The Lorenzian water wheel

This is the first, famous chaotic system discovered by Edward Lorenz, one of the founders of chaos theory, and it is just a lab model of a traditional water wheel.

Imagine a water wheel with buckets and a steady stream of water from the top flowing through holes in the buckets.

If the water flows very slowly, the wheel will never start to rotate as there will not be enough water at one time in the buckets to overcome friction.

If the flow of water is faster, the wheel will start to rotate and it can settle into a steady rate.

But if the flow increases beyond this, the spin can become chaotic. If the spin is too fast, the buckets will not fill up and perhaps also will be too full when they rise on the other side of the wheel. As a result the wheel might slow down and even start to reverse.

Lorenz discovered that, over long periods, the spin can reverse itself many times. The wheel never settles down to a steady rate and it never repeated itself in any predic 'able pattern.

If the relationships had been linear, the spin would eventually have settled down to a predictable pattern. This did not happen as the relationships were non-linear.

If one looks at systems in the short term, and especially if one only looks at small systems, linear relationships can explain much of what we see. The weather forecast for the next day, based on linear or two-dimensional relationships, is usually fairly accurate. For the longer term, or when we look at more complex systems, the limitations of the linear approach become apparent—for instance, the longer term weather forecast is not to be relied upon.

Numerous business decisions are based on reasoning and plans. In almost all situations these plans are based on linear relationships. We take the situation as it is, or was, and project it, logically, on the future. If the plans are for the following week, it is most likely that the decisions and the plans will be correct. If they refer to the following year, the probability that they are correct diminishes dramatically.

EXAMPLE 3.4

The following story (from the *Financial Times*) illustrates the difference between linear and non-linear relationships. 'An Oxford mathematics don who loved animals once bought a Dachshund pup. Every Friday the proud owner fondly weighed and measured his pet, precisely recording its weekly growth. After a few months he took it into the garden of his small house and, with tears in his eye, shot it. He had calculated that in a year's time it would be 27 ft long.'

The arguments above have referred to 'normal' circumstances, if there ever are such situations. If we experience a greater degree of change than previously, the linear reasoning becomes even more flawed and the non-linear effects take over and we get a dynamic, 'chaos', system.

The above presents the first step in non-linear reasoning. The second step is just as important as realizing that non-linear relationships are more important than linear ones. This second part is the discovery that the non-linear relations work as a stabilizing force in a dynamic chaotic system. The non-linear relationships ensure that we do not fall outside the boundaries. If we go too far in one direction, the non-linear feedback systems react and push back so that the system does not get out of control. Non-linearity can, in other words, not only destabilize a system, it can also stabilize it, regulating motion so that it becomes more robust.

The scientists' observations were, mainly, related to physics and biology. In business we deal with human beings, incredibly more complex than studying friction or the weather. This complexity makes non-linearity even more common and it is not unreasonable to assume that all interactions in the business world are based on non-linear relationships.

Boundaries

In the chaos theory framework boundaries take on an important role. The non-linear relationships not only ensure that the systems become unpredictable, they also encourage the system to act within boundaries. Boundaries are, however, not as clear-cut a concept as most would think.

EXAMPLE 3.5

If you look at a coastline from far away it is almost a straight line. A couple of kilometres of coastline on a satellite photograph is, in most cases, easily definable. When you come closer you will see that there are small bays, and creeks and rivers flow out into the ocean changing the shape of the coastline.

If the coast is rocky and you look at just one metre of it, it is far from a straight line. The real length of the coastline is probably two metres, rather than one metre, and full of ins and outs.

If the coastline is a sandy beach, it might still, looking at the one metre stretch, seem a straight line. Taking a look at a one centimetre part of the sandy beach and enlarging that to a metre, we shall see a most uneven coastline, again easily double the length of what we think.

As business people our main concern is not to have a scientifically perfect description of our world. It is much more important to have a way of looking at the world which is operational and a fair approximation of the reality.

I have included this section on boundaries as it illustrates how easy it is to be obsessed with the details of issues and how dangerous it can be to one's perception of the totality to look at sections rather than the whole.

The simple example regarding the coastline also illustrates how important it can be to have the right degree of refinement in one's observations. If the coastline is rocky it is essential to know where the rocks are if one is sailing along the coast and planning to get ashore. If the coast line is sandy all you need to know is an approximation of the location and the depth where you plan to go.

It is worth noting, however, that any approximation that is not based on the reality is useless. Although it is easier to understand the straight coastline than the centimetre of sandy beach, one cannot avoid the fact that if one has not located the centimetre of sandy beach to start with, the approximation is bound to be wrong.

Summary

The purpose of this chapter is not to give a full explanation of chaos theory but rather to bring out a few components that are relevant to business and, in particular, marketing.

The various aspects described will help us build a framework to understand, and above all be more effective in, the marketplace.

Chaos theory as an expression is somewhat misleading as it really refers to three different types of system: stable at the one extreme, uncontrollable at the other with the chaos system in the middle. In the chaos system, variables react irregularly but within boundaries and according to patterns that are unpredictable but regular. Rather than looking at the chaos system as the exception and something that should be avoided, it is in reality the most common and also the most dynamic and the type of system that will generate progress.

The chaos system can survive because the feedback loops are non-linear, as are the functions that build the system in the first place. The non-linearity means that we cannot predict the future with the help of linear equations, but the non-linear aspects serve a double function, giving a dynamic input to the system as well as serving as a stabilizing function, ensuring that the systems stay within the boundaries.

4

Chaos theory and marketing

This chapter will explore how, in principle, the chaos theory concepts in the previous chapter can help us become more effective in marketing our goods and services.

Initially I would like to emphasize that the scientific approach can be no more than a help to our understanding and that the theory cannot be used to predict behaviour, it can only help us understand and suggest a framework.

There is also a risk that if we use such a model too diligently, the analyses will become too mechanical. In marketing we deal with human beings. Regardless of whether the company produces goods for the consumer market or the business-to-business market, the recipient and the decision maker is always a human being. Therefore, emotions, irrationality and unpredictability will always be part of the process.

By looking at the world around us and by using the chaos theory framework our understanding and ability to operate in a changing environment will increase (Figure 4.1). Another effect is that we shall learn to *use* change to our advantage rather than design systems which, intentionally or unintentionally, will restrict change. Larger organizations often have an inbuilt fear of change, and many executives feel threatened by change because they consider that it may undermine their position. This fear is often without foundation, provided the executives involved understand what is happening and why.

It is also worth observing that the size and age of an organization has very little to do with how well it can cope with change. One of the most enduring organizations of all time, the Roman Catholic Church, has survived despite an enormous amount of change in its almost 2000 year history. Whether it will continue to adapt is of course not a matter for this book. New organizations, on the other hand, have a very high mortality rate, although spontaneously one

CHAOS THEORY

Marketing skills

Customers

CHAOS

Marketing theory

Competitors

MARKETING

Management

Change factors

Systems thinking
Feedback loops
Non-repetitive repetitiveness
The nudge effect

Figure 4.1 Using chaos theory to advantage

would have thought that a small and new organization would be extremely adaptable to change, and thus survival.

When the speed of change increases due to technological advances, we need to be even more aware of how we can use this to our advantage, rather than become a victim of what could turn into an uncontrollable system.

Systems thinking

Systems thinking in itself is nothing new, it has been part of business thinking for decades. The relevant point in this context is the realization that the most desirable system is one that is unstable without being out of control—a chaotic system.

In my view the most important conclusion to draw is that it highlights the interaction between company and customer.

Traditionally marketers have been trained to observe the customers, define their needs and wants and then set about fulfilling those needs and wants. The world does not work that way. In a system each action taken generates a feedback, so to stand apart and observe becomes an absurd way of operating. All actions will generate an unpredictable, non-linear response. If a new product is launched, competitors will change their actions, the customers will change their views and perhaps their actions and even the company itself will not be the same after the launch. In other words, the customers are not a 'black box', empty of past history, waiting to be filled with messages and products. Customers are 'living organisms' reacting to information and generating feedback which the original sender of the information should take into account. Actions always generate responses, which raise other responses, and so on.

We can assume, or forecast, that the parts of the system will react in a certain way and it is likely that, if we are experienced anyway, these assumption will be fairly correct. We can also assume, however, that they will not be absolutely correct as that would infer a stable system, something we are unlikely to have.

A further conclusion is that the old saying that 'marketing executives do not create "demand" or "markets"' is simply not true (which most marketers have known in their hearts anyway). If a new, 'good' idea is brought to the market, the customers will buy. The experience of using this product will influence their future views so that the next version of this product will have to take this experience into account in order to continue to be successful. A 'market' has been created, although perhaps not in the way it was intended. For non-marketers one should perhaps add that it is not possible to create a market against the 'will' of the customers: success assumes a positive feedback.

In a market situation it is impossible to isolate the input from the company from the input from the customer, and in the end it does not really matter as the important factor is the interaction between them.

EXAMPLE 4.1

The car industry in Europe has developed in a different way in each major country. It is only in those countries where there has not been a domestic car industry that one can detect a more 'international' and 'general' development (such as Switzerland or Denmark).

In Germany the Autobahn network and lack of speed limits have influenced car engineering and choice of cars.

In France the domestic style of Citroën, Renault and Peugeot has strongly influenced how the French select their cars.

In Italy, half the market is held by Fiat!

In Sweden, Volvo, a premium and niche brand everywhere else in the world, has over 25 per cent of the market, not because of any unique high standard of living in Sweden but because of the interaction between supplier and customers.

In Britain, the narrow roads and, until fairly recently, an underdeveloped motorway system in combination with a tax system that favoured company cars meant, for instance, that luxury cars had to have different features than in Germany.

While the basic 'need' was and is more or less the same in all these countries, the local market conditions, the local marketing systems, have created totally different brand, product and service preferences.

Moving from product to communication this becomes even more relevant. Today's consumers are increasingly active, critical and exposed to more and more communication. Most advertising is still created with no more in mind than a direct response such as increased brand awareness or a trial purchase. Of course, that should remain the objective; there is not much point in advertising a product if the intention or indeed the end result is not that sales will increase.

One has to bear in mind, however, that this is not a one-way street, with the advertiser sending out a message and the customer receiving the message and acting upon it. 'Rather than advertising doing things to people (having "impact", making impressions, hammering home messages), people do things with advertising and brand imagery in order to achieve their goals and ambitions. . . . Even when not actively intending to buy, they assimilate impressions about potential brands for potential future use.' (A. Branthwaite in *The Magazine of the Market Research Society.*)

The advertising issue becomes a true communication issue, i.e. the recipient is no longer passive and even though he or she does not answer back directly, we have similar effects in the mind of the customers. We get brand behaviour effects so that, for instance, a teenager's choice of a plastic carrier bag (with a logo) to carry sports equipment takes on enormous proportions.

EXAMPLE 4.2

The 'New' and 'Classic' Coca-Cola relaunch and launch is a well-known marketing case which illustrates several things, but one issue clearly stands out—the importance of understanding the customers' relationship with the brand.

To recap: Faced with decreasing market share in the US, mainly due to aggressive marketing from Pepsi-Cola, Coca-Cola decided to reformulate Coke to something slightly closer to the Pepsi taste (as Pepsi usually came out slightly ahead in blind tastings). The 'new' Coke recipe went through numerous tests, was generally speaking preferred and was eventually launched. The result was an uproar, the Coca-Cola Company had hurt the feelings of all Coke consumers by changing the taste. The Company had to retreat and relaunched the old recipe as 'Classic' Coca-Cola.

The Coca-Cola consumers resented the fact that the Coca-Cola Company changed 'their' product. The change was imposed on the customers and it was even trumpeted into their ears that this is something NEW, the existing customers did not want anything new, they wanted their 'friend' Coke.

In the author's view the Coca-Cola Company treated the consumers as numbers, disregarding that they had feelings, disregarding that they might react in an unpredictable way, disregarding that they would process the new information and come up with a different conclusion from the company bosses.

The launch of the 'new' Coke was not a product mistake. I believe, on the basis of published material only, that if the changes to the product had been introduced gradually over time as adaptation to the changing tastes (an unquestionable fact) of the US nation, the Coca-Cola Company would not only have avoided a disaster, they would probably today have been in a stronger market position.

The mistake made was in the communication, not the product. The customers, the consumers, were treated without respect and no one likes that. We like to be involved, to feel that we are cared for and that our friends, such as Coke, are on our side.

EXAMPLE 4.3

Heinz Baked Beans, as a product, is almost as old as Coca-Cola and although hardly as glamorous it has, over decades, built a position as a household favourite. Contrary to Coca-Cola, Heinz has succeeded in managing change without losing consumer confidence, and implementing change without getting into an uncontrollable situation.

'Officially' Heinz Baked Beans has only been changed once. That was during the Second World War when pork was taken out of the product, due to rationing.

In reality the product has gone through several changes, the most recent being a reduction in salt and sugar content during the 1980s. These changes were made in order to adapt the product formulation to changing consumer tastes. Heinz never told the consumers of the changes and implemented the changes gradually in order to avoid upsetting their 'valued' customers.

The changes were successful and Heinz Baked Beans remain a best-seller, in 1993, with sales in excess of £100 million.

In jargon, market segments and niches are often referred to as being 'controlled' by brand or company X. This is jargon only and should not be used in any other sense, if at all. The only time a company or an individual can control a market sector is in an environment where the key factors are actually under the real and direct management control of the company. At one stage OPEC was under the impression, along with the rest of the world, that it controlled our oil supplies and thus controlled the oil market. But as we know, this lasted only for a short period. The demand side was not under OPEC control and the situation created by OPEC generated activities in non-OPEC countries so that the apparently stable system was soon undermined.

The oil system remained stable for a short period and is now virtually uncontrollable as the non-linear feedback mechanisms were damaged during the oil crises in the 1970s.

The word 'control' should be banned from marketing as there are very few, if any, factors that a marketing executive can control. It is certainly impossible to control a market sector unless one has total supply monopoly and can at least heavily influence the demand, and very few markets live up to that definition. It is not even possible to control a marketing budget as the competitive situation, and changes to it, has an immediate impact on how marketing resources are spent.

Feedback loops and non-linearity

The feedback loops, negative and positive, play an important role in the marketing context. Our marketing actions generate responses and we need to be aware of these to interpret and take action.

The interpretation of the feedback will be of very limited value unless one recognizes the importance and relevance of non-linearity.

EXAMPLE 4.4

Classic economic theory states that with increased price, demand will decrease. This is not an unusual effect but the relations are virtually always non-linear.

According to the *Financial Times*, over the period 1984–94 the average 'real' price of beer in a pub has risen by 29 per cent and the consumption has fallen by 6 per cent. This in itself is perhaps not surprising but while the price gap increased gradually over the 10 years, the consumption did not start to decrease until 1992/93, the full 6 per cent decline has come in the last two years.

Even the 'simple' price/volume relationship in a large market such as beer is non-linear.

EXAMPLE 4.5

The sales of ice cream lollies and cones is a highly seasonal business. The season really begins when the sun comes out in the spring and tails off in the early autumn. Another market sector where the influence of nature plays a similar role is soft drinks and mineral water: a sunny season is likely to generate a substantial amount of extra sales.

One amazing aspect of this is that early season good weather has a much stronger sales-boosting effect than late season sunshine. A sunny week in May, in particular in the northern part of Europe, can be worth in excess of 20 per cent more in extra sales than a similar period in July.

The consumers' reactions or behaviour in respect of changes to the weather are not really irrational as the behaviour follows what one would expect, i.e. there is a positive relationship between sales and sunshine. The response curve is, however, non-linear in that the strength of the response differs according to how far into the season it is.

The skills required to interpret non-linear reactions are essential to marketing and are often what will differentiate the successful from the mediocre.

Some of the feedback loops are automatic and influence the market system whether we like it or not. Other feedback requires interpretation and will go unnoticed unless someone picks up the information and acts.

In addition some feedback will come into the marketing department virtually without any specific action. For instance, we get sales results back and on the basis of that information we adjust our plans. In order to improve our feedback we might decide to actively search for information and buy market research to understand a bit more of what is going on. Such external information is fed into our systems.

We also have internal loops, such as getting management approval and endorsement, or getting other managers to support the activities we plan.

We cannot operate without these feedback loops and they are crucial in operating the system. What we need to be reminded of by chaos theory is that most, if not all, of these feedback loops are non-linear. Because they are non-linear they are easier to understand the more information we receive. If the information is linear, all we need are two pieces of information and we can calculate the rest. For non-linear relationships we need as much information as we can get and even so we shall never have a full picture as all alternatives have not been tested in real life (if they had been tested, there would be no need for projections).

The conclusion we can draw, however, is that within certain boundaries it is likely that the outcome will be x or y.

Putting the non-linearity together with the systems thinking we get a situation that is very familiar to most marketing executives. We get a number of signals from the market, directly and indirectly, and have to match them with the company systems and values so that the company's market position becomes as strong as possible.

The feedback loops play a very important part as they carry the information that will allow the system to remain within boundaries and be dynamic without being uncontrollable.

Three aspects are of direct importance in this context. The first is the speed of the feedback loop. The sooner the information is collected, the more accurate it will be as it has not been exposed to other changes. At the successful UK car exhaust-fitting company Kwikfit the executives receive every morning full details of the previous day's trading so they can plot key trends.

The second aspect is that the planning horizon becomes shorter. In a non-linear system with a lot of change, long-term planning is obviously an irrelevant occupation. That does not mean that planning horizons disappear. With faster feedback loops, the planning horizon can be shorter and still be effective. The feedback on action taken is picked up and sent back more quickly than before, so the planning cycle can be adapted.

If the planning horizon is not in tune with the total system's response cycle the problems will mount very soon. If one sector of the marketing system has improved its feedback cycle or its sensitivity to it, the other parts will have to do that as well or the boundaries will move and the system might even become uncontrollable.

Over the last decade the information systems in the retail trade have changed dramatically in most part of Europe, scanning and EPOS systems mean that the retailer knows very soon if a product on the shelves is selling or not. In the past it was the manufacturers who knew the sales patterns, based on their own sales figures and consumer panel data.

This change in the feedback systems has not only meant that the retailers have better quality data than anyone else, it has also meant that the manufacturers have been forced to find ways of getting similar information in order not to be totally outplayed and reliant on slow and second-hand feedback systems.

Technology, in addition to being nearer the ultimate customer, has meant that the retailers, as a rule, have greater awareness of emotional and tangible changes in the marketplace.

The net result for the retailers of the improved feedback systems has been that they have strengthened their position in relation to the suppliers and in many instances, especially in the UK, have reached excellent profitability levels.

The third aspect is that planning what to do becomes much less important than planning how to do it. To be able to react quickly to changes, it is important to have a clear picture of what needs to be done. Military commanders place great emphasis on training and exercises so that when the day comes for battle, the troops know how to fight. The training situation is not identical to the real battle but it has provided a way of developing systems for knowing what to do.

Marketing deals to a large extent with humans, and as such we have to be aware of the potentials that open up. As most managers know, positive feedback will generate great results. In the marketing function this is an important aspect of the feedback loops. A positive feedback to, say, a new product should be amplified and put back into the system. The old-fashioned endorsement is nothing but this. You have an individual who expresses his or her delight with a product. Other people hear or see this and get a positive expression, and a positive feedback loop is in action.

EXAMPLE 4.6

During my time as manager in charge of sales and marketing of Nestlé's grocery products in Sweden we launched a new concept in the health food sector: a range of carrot, prune and vegetable juice in a bottle.

The range was put on a test market in one of the major cities. The products achieved good distribution in the retail trade and the launch was supported by outdoor posters. This medium was recommended by the advertising agency as in those days it was the only full-colour medium available in that particular region.

Expectations at the time of launch were high, but sales were disappointing.

Following the 'rule' book a simple piece of market research was carried out to measure penetration and repeat purchases. It turned out that awareness of the range was very low and trial was even less. Out of the sample only a handful of respondents had tried the product. Some important and interesting facts were, however, hidden in the tables. The relationship awareness to purchase was encouragingly high, and of the few who had tried the product 80 per cent had bought again.

We grasped this information and made the decision to revamp the consumer communication programme rather than discontinue the whole range which would have been the obvious result of a disappointing test market. The media was changed from outdoor posters to morning newspapers—never mind the lack of colour—to get to a wider target group at a more appropriate time for the product. A hard-hitting advertisement was created instead of beautiful, colourful pictures. The result of these activities was a sales increase, and within a couple of months the decision was made to go national with the range. Today, over 10 years later, the range is still on the market.

In this case the positive feedback had to be searched for, but once it was found we could eliminate some of the negatives in the marketing mix and go ahead with what was to become a profitable product idea.

Observers are often fascinated by the manner in which large organizations can cope with a changing environment. The above example holds, in my view, one clue. Large organizations have often the capacity to deal with the unexpected; routines are in place, there is a widespread knowledge about what to do and there is a slack in the organization that can deal with the unexpected. The large organizations will only become 'dinosaurs' when they do not understand, act and adapt to the major changes that are happening in their markets.

Non-repetitive repetitiveness

This expression, with its inbuilt contradiction, explains why we get ever-changing results in many marketing activities. The general pattern of the activities we launch is similar from time to time, but the exact results are always more or less different from what is expected.

It is also this concept that explains why experience is so valuable. With time a marketer gets exposure to several versions of similar activities. Experience is built up and with that knowledge his or her ability to judge what is the best way to deploy marketing resources will increase. The boundaries and the patterns will become more obvious as time goes on, although the relevance of the past is dependent on the rate of change.

The variations of the non-repetitiveness differ with the type of system. In a rapidly changing market the variations are, not surprisingly, much wider than in a fairly stable environment. It is, for instance, easier to forecast the outcome of a price promotion of a well-established grocery product such as tea bags than it is to do the same for a range of personal computers or video games.

The 'nudge' effect

The butterfly effect described earlier illustrates the phenomenon that a small change in one part of a system can aggregate into a major change somewhere else because it triggers systems to change.

EXAMPLE 4.7

The frozen food industry went through a great change in 1968 in three countries, Germany, Austria and Italy. In December that year, a joint venture was formed between Unilever and Nestlé to market frozen foods and ice cream. Several years of intense competition was transformed into joint ventures (one in each country) that were to last until 1985.

The result was that Unilever, the larger partner, became the dominant force in frozen foods and ice cream in these countries and today still retains that position. Another effect was that the then joint managing director of Findus Germany (the Nestlé subsidiary), Mr Helmuth Maucher, resigned. He was later re-hired by Nestlé and progressed to become chief executive and chairman of the whole group.

This chain of events, which affected two of the world's largest consumer goods companies and a number of executives' careers, such as Mr Maucher's, was set in motion because one Unilever and one Nestlé senior executive, neither directly involved in the frozen food market in Europe, happened to meet each other on a plane returning from America and started to chat about business issues.

I prefer to call the butterfly effect the *nudge* effect as that is what actually happens in many business situations.

If a system is in a dynamic, chaotic, phase, the feedback loops generate dynamic action within boundaries. If the system is nudged it is possible that the market will change not in a random way but in a desired direction. This can be exploited by the company doing the 'nudging' or, alternatively, a more alert competitor can take the initiative.

Some of these nudges are deliberate and the company involved is aware of what is going to happen. In the consumer goods industry a typical example would be a price war. This can be started by one company deciding that sales are not developing well, and to increase sales the prices are cut. The competitors feel that it is necessary to follow suit and within a week the total price level in a market segment might fall by 10–15 per cent.

EXAMPLE 4.8

IBM and the personal computer market is a well-known business 'disaster' story. Despite technological, financial and selling superiority IBM failed to exploit and dominate the PC part of the computer market.

It is ironic that the PC market was 'nudged' into growth by two IBM-related decisions: one, to develop the MS-DOS system with Microsoft; two, to develop the microchip with Intel. If IBM in 1980 had decided to do this development themselves the PC business and market would be different today. It is even fair to say that as late as 1985 IBM could have changed the course of events (renegotiating the agreements) but by *not* doing something they failed to become a part of a significant market system for the PC market.

Today, despite a relatively large market share, IBM is but a shadow of its former self and suffered in 1992 one of the largest corporate losses in history, $4.97 billion.

One activity in a specific direction, which is picked up and given a positive reception, and exploits the feedback to further increase the activity, can set a whole market sector in motion.

We can take the struggle at one stage between VHS and Betamax video cassettes as a small example. Technically speaking, the two systems were more or less the same—if anything, the Betamax system was slightly better. Because VHS became slightly bigger than Betamax at one crucial stage of the development process, VHS is today the totally dominant system.

Most market systems are in a chaotic and dynamic development.

This means that the company can use the nudge principle to its advantage although it has to be emphasized that one never knows the outcome and it requires fast footwork to be able to pick up the right signals and move along to take advantage of the effects of the nudge.

Planning

In the previous chapter I have explained why sequential planning does not work. The impact of probabilities makes it impossible to get any type of workable document based on a sequence of numbers or events.

Few company executives like to operate totally without planning and marketers are no exception. It is obviously important to have an understanding of the direction in which one would like the business to go. Investments have to be made and in some industries there are lead times that run into years, so a long-term view is essential.

The understanding of how a dynamic system works, the non-linearity and regular irregularities all help in making the right judgements in this area.

The first aspect of this is that one should always aim for as short a planning horizon as possible. The shorter the horizon, the less scope for mistakes and the less risks for the non-linear relationships to play up against the executives.

The second aspect is to plan with alternatives and have a clear understanding of the boundaries. If sales increase by 10 per cent more than planned, what will happen? If they decline rather than increase what will happen? By elaborating on alternative outcomes you get both a greater preparedness to deal with the otherwise unexpected and you get a feel for the boundaries of the internal systems.

The third aspect is that even a non-numerical plan is subject to the chaos system and that a 'vision' or 'mission' which is not based on the core capabilities of the organization is a waste of time (as Professor Kay illustrated in his *Foundations of Corporate Success*). There is conceptually no difference between a numerical or a non-numerical plan; they are both subject to the same dynamic system and are equally likely to be considered outdated before they are written.

EXAMPLE 4.9

One of the first companies in Europe to officially abandon long-term planning was a Swedish bank, Svenska Handelsbanken. By the 1970s the planning function had already been thrown out. Under the dynamic leadership of Dr Wallander, Svenska just refused to publish any forecasts beyond what was absolutely necessary. The efforts were instead directed towards understanding the marketplace, ensuring that the cost structure was as competitive as possible, core competences developed and that credit risks were properly managed.

This strategy has been followed ever since and it is significant that during the Scandinavian financial crisis in the early 1990s the only Swedish bank to survive without any form of government support was Svenska.

The shortcomings of the planning process are not an excuse for poor planning or no planning at all. Attention to detail and awareness of options are always very important. The negative, unforecastable effect of non-linearity can be reduced by ensuring that executives are totally aware of these aspects. As a famous golfer said: 'The more I practise, the luckier I get.'

A planning process that is based on defining the core capabilities of an organization, the competitive advantages and the required skills to survive in the marketplace will have positive benefits. A process that serves to produce suggested actions for the next 12 or 24 months is unlikely to be useful unless the plans are sufficiently open to exploit the feedback.

Boundaries

When looking at a market segment or a customer profile one can easily get too involved in details: 'You can't see the wood for the trees.' The example of the coastline in the previous chapter illustrates the problems connected with correctly defining the boundaries.

The boundaries provide the limits within which the system reacts in a more or less unpredictable way. The repetitiveness within the boundaries is what makes experience a very valuable commodity. Although the exact pattern is unpredictable in a dynamic system, a generally approximate pattern is likely to develop through repetition.

With technological progress we not only get more change, we also get more information. This information can be very useful but it can also confuse. To have an adequate understanding of feedback and to have a proper view of the boundaries of customer systems, the marketer needs to look at data from a correct distance: too close and the main conclusions will not be seen; too far away and there will be a lack of understanding of what is really happening.

Summary

This chapter has highlighted some of the aspects of marketing in a changeable world. The most important aspect of this is not that there is a lot of change in the market place—there always has been change, more or less depending on circumstances; the important issue is that to succeed you have to recognize change as the 'normal' situation.

The interactive systems—the positive and negative feedback loops, the non-linearity in almost everything we do and the fuzzy boundaries to our activities—are all important aspects that will influence the effectiveness of marketing.

5

Chaos marketing: key strategies

In this chapter I shall introduce strategies and concepts that will help the marketing executive to win in the volatile and in many instances turbulent business world.

Recognizing that the environment will always change is the first step to successful marketing in a dynamic environment. Knowing what to do and how to do it in order to succeed is the next and the main challenge. Major factors causing change, such as more rapid flow of communications and technological advances in computing and telecommunications, are not to be regarded as nuisances causing unwanted change. They can be used to boost prosperity if the marketers are aware of, and have the ability to recognize, the key factors.

One might be discouraged by the unpredictability of a chaos system and frustrated by the apparent random changes to our environment. With the help of a few chaos concepts we can better learn from experience and more easily understand that the turbulence opens up opportunities for those who realize what is going on and have the skills to exploit the situation. Those who understand and are aware automatically have a head start on the competition.

The essential ingredients for business success

Prior to getting too involved in the real marketing issues, a look at how corporate success comes about will add a dimension to our understanding of how to achieve success.

In the author's view the best, recent, book on the subject of key factors for business success is Professor Kay's *Foundations of Corporate Success*. Four distinct capabilities are defined in the book as reasons for success: *architecture, reputation, innovation* and *strategic assets*.

The first aspect, architecture, refers to how an organization is run: the management processes. In a marketing context this relates not only to decision-making processes but also to the implementation of marketing decisions, the management of the marketing departments and related functions, etc. These issues will be dealt with later in the book.

The second aspect, reputation, reflects in brand and product loyalty. The brand represents the reputation of a company or product, and to create and build that reputation by managing the various elements of the marketing mix is, of course, a key task for a marketer.

The third aspect, innovation, is, like branding, a core marketing activity. While innovation as such comes from all kinds of sources, it is the exploitation of the innovation that creates wealth. Our history is full of inventions (the transistor, the VCR, the quartz) that have failed to become innovations for the inventors.

The fourth capability, to have strategic assets, is not often an issue of relevance to the marketer. Strategic assets are, for instance, legal monopolies such as water services or total dominance due to very high entry costs such as the generation of electricity in nuclear power plants. It is well worth being aware of this factor, however, as it is not unusual that turbulence is created by strategic assets being undermined. Government decisions to break up companies or to take away monopolies create dynamic and chaos systems out of fairly stable situations—the partial break-up of the brewery–pub link in the UK being a typical example. As the breweries can no longer fully control the distribution of beer to the ultimate consumer, the competitive parameters have changed and the system is becoming more 'chaotic' and dynamic. If the marketer does not realize that the reason for a certain profit level is that the company sits on strategic assets, serious misjudgements can take place.

Despite the fact that change is all around us, these capabilities do take time to build. Reputations are rarely built overnight; innovations are more often than not based on 5 per cent inspiration and 95 per cent perspiration; successful and efficient company architecture takes several years to build; and, of course, strategic assets are usually the result of a historic situation. These capabilities, however, can quite easily and quite quickly be destroyed and one aspect of this, which as a marketer one must never forget, is that actions taken in order to gain ground in the marketing war must never ruin the capabilities that take time to create and are essential for success.

This very brief summary of a few aspects of the *Foundations of Corporate Success* does highlight the direct influence of marketing in two key capabilities: reputation and innovation. The understanding of the importance of architecture and strategic assets is also of great use for the creation and management of a successful and winning marketing strategy.

Marketing as a system: stability and turbulence

All actions we take are part of a system and the market we deal with is no exception. All aspects or dimensions of that system have, or can have, a dynamic effect. If we change a part of the marketing mix we expect something to happen; if prices are increased or decreased it is likely that the customers and the competitors will react. If we run a sales promotion the purpose is to create dynamism, changes to customer behaviour.

Reviewing the various parts of the marketing mix it becomes apparent that each type of activity has a more or less stabilizing or destabilizing effect on the relationship between company and (potential) customer. It is, however, quite possible that the induced reaction/response from competitors can trigger changes that we have not anticipated.

Availability ('Place' of the classical four marketing Ps), is a factor that usually stabilizes a system. If a product or service is easily accessible for the customer, sales and relationships stabilize. Companies that totally control the physical distribution of their product—for instance, an electrical power supplier—usually operate in a very stable environment. The British brewers had in the past full control of the distribution chain, effectively depriving newcomers of a foothold in the on-trade.

Communication in respect of building intangible values that increase the brand loyalty also have a stabilizing effect, although less so than availability. The big consumer brands such as Nescafé and Coca-Cola have, over the years, shown remarkable stability, at least partly because of advertising strengths.

EXAMPLE 5.1

A report by S. Knox of Cranfield School of Management and L. de Chernatony of City University compared two drinks markets, still mineral water and fruit juices, in three leading multiple retailers in the London area.

During the period 1983–89 the advertising spend on still mineral water grew by 720 per cent to £7.1 million while the spend on fruit juice declined by 60 per cent to £3.2 million.

In 1989 the brand shares were such that the leading still water brand had a share of 19 per cent, compared with a combined 26 per cent for the own labels, while the leading juice brand had a share of 10 per cent, compared with 63 per cent for the own labels.

The price difference between the leading three brands in relation to the own labels was that in the mineral water sector the price premium enjoyed by the branded products over the own labels was 22 per cent while in the fruit juice market the premium was just 1 per cent.

In the market sector where the advertising spend was higher, the advertised brands enjoyed a higher share and a higher price and the own-label sector had taken less share than in the low spend market sector.

Reviewing the other end of the activity spectrum, if a market sector is bombarded with (relevant) technical innovations, such a market is usually destabilized. Over the last decade most parts of the electronics market would qualify as illustration to this statement. Of the top 10 semiconductor manufacturers in 1983 only six remained in the top in 1993. Looking at individual companies, Applied Materials was No. 7 in 1983 and No. 1 in 1993, Tokyo Electron was No. 9 in 1983 and No. 2 in 1993, while Canon, No. 4 in 1993, was not even among the top 10 in 1983.

Another destabilizing factor is promotions—in particular, price-related promotions. Price wars can lead to systems running out of control and becoming totally unpredictable.

The personal computer market, in particular in the early 1990s, represented a combination of these two aspects. With technical innovation (such as new models with higher-performance chips) and price reductions (the average price fell by 30 per cent between 1991 and 1992), the market was in a most volatile phase, and from time to time was almost totally out of control.

Real and lasting supplier-initiated change in a market sector has usually come about due to (1) the aggressive marketing of a new product (in the widest sense of the word), (2) an apparent revolution in one part of the supply chain, or (3) a combination of the two.

An example of the first is the introduction of the video camera, which totally changed the 'home-film' market. An entire industry based on the 8-mm film disappeared within a few years and was replaced by the electronic equivalent, the camcorder. It is well worth noting, however, that the market change did not take place until the manufacturers, the Japanese giants such as Sony and JVC, introduced a technology that was easy to use and was available at a price that made the camera affordable to a wider audience.

An example of the second—changes to the supply chain—can be seen in the operation of discount retailers such as ALDI in Germany. The success of ALDI has changed not only the price levels and profitability of the total retailing market in Germany, but also the shopping patterns and brand positions. The presence and appeal of ALDI has meant that the price level is very low; the profitability of the retailers is much lower than in, for instance, the UK with the additional effect that subjectively the stores are under-invested, multi-stop shopping is more common (ALDI carries only a limited range) and the pricing variable in the marketing mix is of greater importance than in many other countries.

Finally, the third option, which is a combination of (1) and (2), can be represented by IKEA, one of the world's largest furniture retailers. It has in many countries totally changed furniture retailing by selling furniture with distinct and attractive design, packed in flat packs for self-assembly at a very low price and often in an unorthodox way.

While the rapid introduction of technical innovations can cause instability, careful development of existing products leads to stability. The relationship between brand and customer is a dynamic system, and to remain manageable the product and the brand image need to move with the changes in the target group. The effects of one part falling behind in the change process will be that the dynamic stability is rocked, the rate of change and instability may increase and the brand/product might lose its position.

One reflection in this context is that the more 'uncontrolled' change that many consumer goods companies have felt threatened by over the last decade is, to a certain degree, self-inflicted. Over the last 10–15 years there has been a change in the marketing mix from the stabilizing factors, such as communication, to the destabilizing ones, such as price promotions and new product development. The spend on price promotions has increased, both in total and in relation to traditional advertising, and the number of new products launched has increased substantially—for instance, in the United States the number of new food and beverage products launched each year has grown from around 3000 in the early 1980s to around 10 000 a decade later.

It has always been important to understand how the actions of a company influence the marketplace. In a more turbulent environment this becomes essential. By understanding what dimensions or variables cause a system to change, the marketer will not only have a greater ability to predict that what he or she is planning will actually happen, but also be able to understand why and what the consequences might be.

Elements of the marketing mix

In the following list the elements of the marketing mix are ranked according to how they can influence stability:

Most turbulent

- Totally new products
- Price change
- Product innovation (new product development)
- Sales promotion
- Product enhancement (old product development)
- PR and other forms of non-advertising communication
- Advertising
- Personal selling

Most stabilizing

- Own distribution system

Evaluating the marketplace

The previous section dealt mainly with factors that the company or the marketing department can manage and influence. The market system is, of course, also influenced by external factors, which can be categorized in five groups:

- Competitors
- Governments
- Social change
- Technological change
- Nature.

From a marketing point of view the main concern in this context is to understand how the external factors will influence the customers' behaviour, although one has also to consider the influence that external factors can have on the company and its competitors (see Figure 5.1).

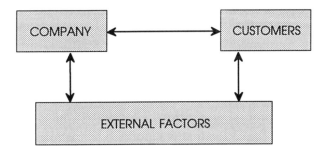

Figure 5.1 The interrelationships

For instance, the marketing activities of a tobacco company are heavily influenced by the fact that external factors (governments) have restricted the use of the marketing mix by not allowing advertising.

External factors can influence the market in two different ways: first, by inducing changes to the total demand; secondly, by altering the relative strength of a brand/company.

The changes imposed by governments on the tobacco industry influences (at least in theory) the total market, while competitive activities will change the brand shares of each company. For instance, in 1993 the discount part of the cigarette industry in the US lost market share because of the price activities taken by Philip Morris/Marlboro (Chapter 6).

Some factors have a more general effect than others. For instance, if the sun shines the whole of the ice-cream and drinks industry benefits, not only certain brands. Equally, as indicated above, government activities usually are aimed at total market sectors, leaving the relative strengths more or less unchanged.

Of the five categories listed above, the one that concerns most marketers is *competition*. Competitors affect the way a company operates in a market sector, but they also affect the customers directly, i.e. their attitudes and habits. The competitor's market system—i.e. the relationships between that company and the common target group—influences the customers. Almost everyone who has tried to enter a new region has experienced that the customers react differently than in the 'home' market, because they have been accustomed to another set of competitive parameters and have adapted accordingly. The car industry in Europe is a prime example (Chapter 4).

The influence of governments has been commented upon above. Government activity changes from country to country and from market sector to market sector. The influence does not have to be negative as regulations can be to a company's advantage, and if a company is selling something that the government supports, the company in question might benefit from government propaganda. One such example is products developed in order to help individuals to stop smoking. These products clearly benefit from the anti-smoking information that is supported by many governments.

Social change is a very general force but one that every marketer has to be, and usually is, aware of. Some elements of social change are well documented, such as changes to the family structure and number of children per family. Other aspects, such as attitudes to sports or healthy eating, might be more difficult to get a real and thorough understanding of as the mass media does not necessarily reflect the view of the general public and perhaps even less so a company's specific target group.

Technological change, on the other hand, is quite apparent. We can measure and review how a specific target group is accepting new technology, particularly relevant in industrial goods marketing, and draw our conclusions. In most cases it is not the technology as such that is of the greatest interest, it is the impact of the technological changes on other product usages and general habits.

The impact of nature on target customers is not something that is disappearing with the advent of technology. In some instances we are now more vulnerable to unexpected natural events than previously as we have built an increased dependence on, for example, electricity, telecommunications and convenient food and water supplies. If any of these are interrupted, the effects on the marketplace can be dramatic—the earthquake in Los Angeles being a prime example. It is, however, not only in such dramatic circumstances that nature has an influence on the market system. Sunshine or rain does make a difference to the consumption of many consumer goods and attitudes to heating systems, for instance, certainly change with the climate.

All these activities have an impact on the rate of change in a market sector. While change is normally seen as a move towards instability this does not necessarily follow. For example, if a government introduces legislation to restrict the use of pricing as a competitive weapon, i.e. enforcing equal price to all customers, it will stabilize a market.

The marketing executive needs to assess how turbulent a market sector really is prior to deploying the marketing mix resources. The degree of turbulence needs to be assessed in a fairly objective way in conjunction with defining how and why the dimensions are changing. This analysis is of importance when it comes to choosing the strategy (see later this chapter) and determining the parts of the marketing mix to focus on.

In theory one can spend a lot of time doing such an analysis but in reality any experienced business person can quite quickly grasp the pace of change. The factors that determine the pace are also in most cases quite apparent. A simple statement to describe whether a market sector is in a fairly stable, dynamic, rapid change or in an uncontrollable state is usually sufficient, with a list of the key change variables listed in the same context.

A more interesting and challenging analysis is to look at the potential for external change (Figure 5.2). Within the categories listed above, is there a potential for change? In most cases the answer is 'yes' and the thought process required for reaching that conclusion will be most useful not only to make you more aware of

---

Market sector: ....

Current situation: ....

Level of change: stable ....
                       fairly stable ....
                       dynamic......................
                       rapid change ....
                       out of control..............

Key variable(s) causing change: dimension x................................
                                     dimension y ....

Potential situations: Key change dimension(s) by category (list at least one by category):

	Dimension	Effect
Competitors	....	....
Governments	....	....
Social change	....	....
Technological change	....	....
Nature	....	....

Figure 5.2 Market change analysis

what might come but also to enable you to lay the foundations for a strategy that *uses* change to gain competitive advantage.

Going through the process of defining the level of dynamism in the market system and the main current and potential change dimensions, the ground work is in place for a review of the potentials for using change as a way of surviving in a dynamic marketplace.

Principles for winning strategies

Just by understanding change the marketer has gained a competitive advantage. It makes the executive aware of the potential problems and opportunities. By using change the understanding is transformed into winning strategies.

It is quite obvious that the same strategy is not the best for everyone. The main difference lies between those companies and brands that are in a leading situation and wish to protect themselves and gain from a position of strength and those who have an inferior position and are challenging the established brands.

The two strategies are conceptually different, which explains why so many brand-leading companies often have problems with aggressively building a business in a 'challenger' role.

The brand leader strategy

The optimal situation for a brand leader is a system that is in fairly slow dynamic change. Judging from companies that have, over time, managed to lead and stay in the lead, the successful level of change has been one of moderation.

Companies that do not change and aim for a stable environment will soon be challenged (unless the strategic assets are so strong that the stability remains unchallenged) and if they do not have the ability to change they will disappear. Top consumer brands such as Nescafé, Andrex, Flora and Heinz Baked Beans survive and prosper because they change, but not at too rapid a speed. As a contrast General Motors lost its, at one stage 'unassailable', market position because it did not respond to change and IBM lost its position because the market went into a very rapid change while the company didn't. The only hardware computer company to have a reasonable track record over the last five years is Apple, because it has managed change by being much more skilful in handling the stabilizing dimensions such as communication and product enhancement. On the other hand, Levi's, one of today's top marketing companies, expanded in the 1970s and developed in all kinds of directions with disastrous results. Levi's has also demonstrated that it is possible to bring back a business from an almost uncontrollable situation to a manageable dynamic rate of change.

The examples mentioned above are just illustrations. No system is totally stable and particularly from a marketing point of view, dealing with human beings influenced by everything around us, it is absurd to assume that stability is even possible.

At the other end of the spectrum, with change that is out of control, it is unlikely that a current or past brand leader will win. By definition, a system that is out of control will not come back to anything close to the position it held previously. Consequently, an out-of-control system is undesirable or even dangerous for the survival of a company, and in particular a company with a leading position.

Of the two extremes, for an established company it is possible that the stable situation is slightly less dangerous than the out-of-control one. The reason is that in a non-dynamic situation you will retain some core capabilities which you can easily push into a more dynamic scenario, while if the market is out-of-control it can be very difficult to save a company and get it back into some sort of manageable situation.

Having ruled out the two extremes, the options left are in the dynamic, chaos system. Such a system can go through rapid change or slow change, depending on the activities of the proactive parts of the system (the suppliers), the respondents (the customers) and the external forces (government, nature, social change, etc.). The slower the change process, the easier it becomes to manage; just by having more time to respond helps so that subsequent evaluations and actions can be better thought through. It is also true that the larger the company's influence in a market sector (and that is as a rule in proportion to the market share) the greater the ability to guide the change process.

This analysis, in combination with practical experience, indicates that for a brand leader the ultimate position is one of slow dynamic change, keeping up or slightly exceeding the pace of change in behaviour among the key decision makers. A successful route for long-term prosperity is a strategy that nurtures change and slowly pushes the development forward, keeping one step ahead of the external forces in order to keep the initiative and ensuring that the volatile dimensions of the marketing mix are tightly managed. This does not suggest, however, that to succeed as a brand leader one should slow down! It is only by assessing the market situation that one can determine whether it is in a company's interest to aim for an increase or decrease to the pace of change.

The challenger strategy

In this situation the strategy has to be different. After all, Microsoft's Bill Gates did not become a multibillionaire by imitating IBM! A challenger has a lot to gain from a more volatile environment as it opens up opportunities at a more rapid pace and those opportunities might be more 'crazy' than in a more stable system.

The strategy has to take into account the capabilities of the challenging organization. The more solid the architecture, reputation and ability to innovate, the better is the ability to manage in a more dynamic system. With a high ability to introduce relevant innovations, and with a strong brand image and an organizational structure that can cope and respond to new opportunities more quickly than the other players in the market, a company can become No. 1 when the market system has moved from slow dynamic change to rapid change.

A challenger strategy based on destabilizing factors, such as price promotions and new product development, is more likely to be successful (in relation to costs) than one based on stabilizing factors such as advertising and product enhancement. For instance, the long-term positive effects of price promotions have only been proved in one particular situation—when introducing a new product.

Also, in a more chaotic environment the 'nudge' factor will have greater relative impact. In rapid change, the multiplier effect will work much faster than in a stable environment. The 'nudge' factor is particularly useful for a challenger as you can achieve much with limited resources, and the risks that it will go wrong are less for a company with a limited stake in a market than for one with a large stake.

A more dynamic marketplace is also to the advantage of the challenger for the very simple reason that it is to the disadvantage of the brand leader. If the brand leader is likely to gain from *slow* dynamic change, the challenger will, of course, gain from *rapid* dynamic change.

The rapid change strategy can have two origins. First, in the case of a proactive strategy the company decides to enter a market segment and to unsettle the brand leader. To gain a competitive advantage it deploys a marketing mix that leads to rapid change. Secondly, a company can analyse a market sector and in doing so realize that the market is moving into a much more dynamic phase or instability. On the basis of this instability, it can enter the market and exploit the new situation.

The increased pace of change in recent years in many parts of the business world has not only been fuelled by technological and social forces. The change in marketing budgets from 'stabilizing' advertising to 'destabilizing' price promotions has certainly played a part in transforming the marketplace. According to a survey of 300 US firms by Myers Marketing & Research (a New Jersey based consultant) the companies allocate more than two-thirds to promotions and one-third to advertising. Ten years ago the situation was the reverse: two-thirds advertising and one-third promotions.

Dell's challenge to the personal computer market is one example of using price and technical innovation to gain market share in combination with a new distribution system (mail order) in order to by-pass the previously main stabilizing factor in the market place, the dealerships. In just 10 years Michael Dell of Austin, Texas has built a company from nothing to become the world's fifth largest personal computer company. Just one changing external force, the PC becoming a consumer product rather than a business one, was used and enforced with very profitable results.

The rise of discount chains (such as Kwiksave and ALDI) in food and drink retailing is another example of using the price dimensions to gain a strong market position against the traditional supermarkets.

Implications

My main reason for highlighting the two different strategies is that we often take standard solutions to solve problems or exploit opportunities. In reality we are much more likely to be successful if we adapt the strategy and our use of the marketing mix not only to our core capabilities but also to the amount of change in the market and the amount of change we would like to see in a market.

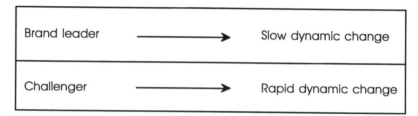

Figure 5.3 Principal strategies

For a brand leader it can be disastrous if the pace of change is misunderstood and the wrong means are used for retaining the market position. For instance, using new product development and price cutting as a key plank, rather than old product development and advertising, is not in most cases a good approach.

The suggested brand leader strategy also illustrates that not to change is almost as bad a strategy as one of throwing the market into an out-of-control situation. For a challenger, the most cost-effective approach is challenging a brand leader to aim for destabilizing the market and move it into rapid change. Such a change can be caused by external forces and/or be pushed by the challenger (Figure 5.3).

In both cases one must also remember that activities to stabilize and destabilize are not guaranteed to succeed, rather the reverse. The deployment of marketing resources will only push, 'nudge', the development in a certain direction. The nudge might multiply as planned or it might lead to nothing at all. A dynamic system is *not* predictable.

Regardless of the situation for a company or a brand, it becomes essential to understand the effects of change and how to manage the various elements. Both types of companies or brands will benefit from change. If they can use the system and survive in it, it is 'just' a question of using and influencing the various dimensions to achieve the best results. It is also worth noting that as long as the system is not out of control it is possible to influence, it but we can *never* be sure of how the system will react to our actions.

Example 5.2

During the 1980s the Nestlé company in the UK managed the Nescafé range of products with such skill that the company became the subject of a Monopolies and Merger Commission report in 1989. The product is also an excellent case of how change can be managed by a brand leader, to the detriment of the challengers.

During the 1980s the Nestlé products gained 10 percentage points in brand share, so that by the end of the decade the share was 58 per cent, a very dominant position for a grocery product. The share growth was achieved despite a number of challenges from other branded products such as Brooke Bond's Red Mountain, General Food's Maxwell House and, in particular, low-priced own-label products.

The reason for the success was a combination of product development (using better coffee beans and better processing) and more effective advertising without allowing the price differentials to become too large. The stabilizing factors—advertising and product enhancement—were used to counter destabilizing activities, own-label coffees selling at less than half price and competitors launching several new products.

It is of interest to note that the origin of the product enhancement strategy was a rapid change in the raw material market. In the late 1970s the price of raw coffee increased dramatically and in the early 1980s it declined. These changes, in particular the latter, were used to enhance the product quality, transforming a potentially very unsettling situation into one of building slow dynamic change.

The defensive options

The above has been in virtually all instances based on the perspective of taking the proactive part in the competitive scenario. In many cases a company faces a competitive threat which restricts the parameters in the sense that the initiative is outside the company's control and a plan of action has to take into account the changes that the challenger has initiated.

The 'easy' answer to this issue is to ensure that the market position is so strong and that the marketing programme is sufficiently proactive to deter any aggressor. Unfortunately the situation is rarely that comfortable.

When a company is facing a challenge the first analysis has to be to determine whether the threat is real and whether it 'deserves' a specific strategy. For a brand leader it can be counter-productive to counter all competitive threats, as by doing so the main thrust of the company will be diluted.

The first conclusion is that the primary line of defence is to ensure that the company is in as strong a position as possible and that feedback systems are in place to monitor the development of the total competitive situation.

If the attack is considered a real threat the company has two alternative marketing strategies: it can neutralize the attack by countering the challenger on the same terms, such as matching a price offer or launching a similar product; or it can enhance the company's own marketing programme and build on stabilizing factors.

If the former strategy is chosen the basic rule is that it is essential to hit as soon as possible, the attack must be 'killed' at an early stage as the longer the defender waits, the more difficult it will be to erase the challenger from the marketing system. This is particularly true if the challenge is based on a price platform and a company has chosen to defend on that platform. If the challenge consists of a 'new' product offer, the defender might have a little more time but, on the other hand, creating the defence, i.e. developing a me-too product, might be a lengthy process. In both cases the defence must be targeted as otherwise other parts of the system might suffer unnecessarily.

The second conclusion is that the sooner a challenger's offer is met, the better.

The main concern for a leading brand, regardless of the type of challenge, must be that it should never lose the position of being the leading influence in the market system in question. If the main initiative transfers to a challenger, the commercial situation can deteriorate rapidly.

Summary

The general strategy in a dynamic and changing environment is different for a brand leader than for a challenger, but in either case the corporation will benefit from change provided that the marketing activities are planned and implemented with this in mind.

In the case of a brand leader, an approach that is based on slow dynamic change is likely to be the most profitable, while a challenger will benefit more from a rapidly changing market system.

A totally stable system is almost an impossibility, considering that marketers deal with human nature. At the other end of the spectrum, very few companies benefit from an out-of-control market.

The marketer can deploy the marketing mix variables with this in mind, using stabilizing factors such as advertising, or destabilizing ones such as new product innovations, in order to achieve the best possible results. It will also help the company's ability to take the right action if it has a clear picture of the level of chaos in the brand's marketing system and is aware of those factors that might trigger volatile change.

PART THREE

THE OPERATIONAL ASPECTS OF CHAOS MARKETING

It is always essential to realize that no strategy will work unless it is implemented effectively. If the pace of change in the environment is on the increase, then effective implementation becomes even more important as there is less time to correct mistakes and chase the weak links of the operational chain, and the multiplier and non-linear effects will happen even more rapidly.

The main difference for the marketer is that the traditional emphasis on planning 'what to do' *and* 'how to do it' must change to a focus on planning 'how to do it' and keeping the options open regarding 'what to do' until as late as possible. The executional options can be considered well in advance of any decision, but the later the commitment to expenditure is made, the more likely it is that the background information for the decision makers is relevant and applicable also at the time of implementation.

The relevance of this was dramatically highlighted by the Japanese success stories during the 1970s and 1980s. The speed of implementation was a crucial factor, and the famous example of the Japanese car industry requiring half the time of Western companies to develop a new model was a case in point. Other organizations have realized this and Unilever's chairman, Mike Perry, was quoted in *Marketing* magazine as saying: 'We want ... [to] create the brand and move it around the world at the marketing equivalent of the speed of light.'

It is also important to realize that adaptation and change do not necessarily mean that 'everything' has to change; successful operations evolve and change with the system, but if all aspects are changed the system and company itself will become one that is out of control. Consistency in consumer communication, as demonstrated with great skills by brands such as Andrex, Mars and

Levi's, can overcome some of the market turbulence while rigidity, for instance, in pricing structures or trade relations can cause great problems.

6

Monitor and modify

The significance of feedback loops

In traditional management textbooks much emphasis is put on planning. As has been proved on many occasions, it is almost impossible to plan what will happen in the future and the increased volatility in the marketplace has meant that medium and long-term planning is becoming even more irrelevant. Instead the conclusion is that it is much more essential to monitor the market and modify the company's performance, in the widest sense of the word, to ensure that the company is actually moving ahead in the right direction and that the very beneficial but often small adjustments are made constantly. The chaos system should be given small pushes, modified, to move in the desired direction.

To be able to monitor what is happening in the marketplace with the competitors and in the company it is essential to have feedback loops in place. These can be informal and/or part of the management system.

Regarding the overall market situation it is worth repeating that it is essential to be aware of the *real* pace of change and not be misled by hyped-up newspaper articles and conference presentations or by non-receptive traditionalists and representatives of the status quo.

All systems have feedback loops but if the marketer is not aware of them, or ignores them, the brand will not survive as he or she will not give the right input to adapt to all the changes in the systems.

The formal feedback loops include sales and market statistics, sales reports, customer complaints reports, market research reports, surveys of customer attitudes, etc. All these exist in most companies but if they are to be of value three criteria have to be fulfilled: (1) they have to be recognized; (2) they have to be produced in a format that is easily digestible and relevant to the business, and (3) they have to be 'fresh'. The faster the pace of change in the marketplace, the faster the feedback must be!

When companies fail to discover a trend in the marketplace it is not because the feedback loops have not been in place, it is because the signals have not been correctly interpreted or acted upon.

EXAMPLE 6.1

One of the more dramatic of such cases in recent years is Philip Morris and Marlboro in the US, once upon a time an unassailable brand marketer. Philip Morris got so confident of its own brand strengths that the company chose to ignore the rise of the cheaper brands and pushed its own perception of the Marlboro value for money too far.

Over a decade discounter-brands rose from 0 to 30 per cent market share while at the same time Marlboro's retail price, along with the retail prices of other premium brands, had been pushed up by an annual average of +11 per cent, well ahead of inflation. All went well until 1990 when it was just pushed a little bit too far (relatively speaking) and the brand share started to decline from the all-time high of 1989 when Philip Morris had 42 per cent of the domestic market with Marlboro at over 26 per cent. The consumers started to react, the market share started to fall and in 1992 it was no longer over 26 per cent but just under 24.5 per cent. To the credit of Philip Morris it took the only reasonable route to quickly reverse the situation, cutting the price by up to 20 per cent to restore the value for money perception.

The cut was dramatic, especially when considering the impact it had on the bottom line, but necessary. It is probably also true that had the cut been made before, or had the company been less arrogant in its pricing policy earlier on, the total loss of profits would have been significantly less. And the advertising budget of over $100 million was not sufficient to overcome the changed perception of the real value.

By the time Philip Morris was announcing its 1993 results to the stock markets, the company could also announce that it had managed to 'regain market share in the premium category'.

Over the last decades there has been a change of emphasis in the consumer goods industry from the manufacturers to the retailers, as mentioned previously. There are many structural reasons for this and one is the improved flow of information from the shops. In the past, information was based on stock movements; today it is based on consumer purchases. With a proper system such information can easily and quickly be at the disposal of the managers involved in range and pricing policies and they can react with immediate effect. Operations with accurate and fast information feedback loops have a distinct advantage.

The informal or qualitative feedback loops are also important. Talking to customers, reading statements and observing what is going on from a subjective point of view can give suggestions and ideas that can improve the functioning of the system and improve the relative competitive advantage.

When taking in the information from the feedback loops and also observing how the system reacts to the information, patterns will emerge. These patterns will tell the marketer what he or she can expect from the system in the future and build up an understanding of the dynamics of the marketplace. This makes experience a more useful commodity in a changing world than otherwise, as someone with experience is more likely to analyse the patterns correctly.

This reasoning has been made from the view point of the company and the marketer. The system works, of course, the other way as well. The automatic feedback loops feed into the marketplace and trigger various forms of reactions. A new advertising campaign will, probably or hopefully, influence the customers who might change their behaviour and/or views. That change will influence further actions among all competitors and so the system continues to provide feedback in both directions.

EXAMPLE 6.2

Findus UK produces and markets a successful range of frozen snack products called Crispy Pancakes. I was in charge of this product group for a period when I was marketing manager for Findus. True to the prevailing attitudes at the time, our main concern was to find new products to extend the range of Crispy Pancakes and the product idea we suggested was Wholemeal Crispy Pancakes. A launch decision was made and a fairly substantial launch budget was allocated.

We very soon realized that the product concept was not going to be a success so rather than continue with the idea and spend more money to support it, the advertising funds were shifted to the standard range.

The result was that with the extra advertising support, the standard Crispy Pancakes grew in volume and the input of extra money set in motion a chain of events that eventually led to the doubling of the business.

By monitoring and modifying, the company reaped considerable benefits although the original reason for the extra funding was soon forgotten!

Especially in larger corporations it is essential to be aware of the 'political' implications of monitoring and modifying. A management group who has heavily committed itself to one set of actions, can find itself in a situation where monitoring works but it becomes internally difficult to modify. The organization needs to be open and 'forgiving' if it is to survive. It must be possible to change the structure or the strategy that was agreed at a budget meeting or at a head office review.

Feedback systems also react, of course, on false information. Companies, and perhaps in particular sales and marketing executives, have been known to spread information that is incomplete or even wrong, sometimes deliberately and sometimes just out of lack of awareness of the real situation. The system reacts either way, but as always with a dynamic system you can never be too sure about how the system will react!

On more than one occasion test markets by FMCG companies have been skewed by competitive activity, such as special price promotions or special features in order to reduce the sale of the product on test. One company in the paper tissue market used a different tactic during a test launch by a competitor in the 1970s. The tactic was to 'sabotage' the competitor's test market by buying up all stock in the test stores immediately at the launch. In doing so all results were biased in that the shelves were empty, no significant consumer trial was generated and repeat purchases became impossible. The activity was successful in that the competitive product never was launched nationally.

As we are increasingly relying on technology to produce data summaries, often in attractive graphical formats, it is worth reiterating that the accuracy of the data one is monitoring is never better than the source.

It has been stated above that the feedback system needs to be fast. How fast depends on several factors. First, the feedback needs to be at least as fast as that of the competition, if not the competitive standing will suffer. Secondly, it needs to be at least as fast as the changes in the marketplace. Thirdly, the company's ability to pick up the feedback needs to be as fast as that of the customers.

Summary

It is worth noting that the market system has a number of feedback loops that react totally independently of any marketing executive's interpretation and actions. For instance, if a product does not sell, orders will not be sent and sales will tail off. Such a feedback loop can generate all kinds of actions, some influenced by marketers, such as promotions to increase sales, others by other company executives, such as pulling back on production, and another effect might be that a distributor decides to delist the product, a decision totally outside the marketer's sphere of influence.

All systems function with the help of feedback. Sometimes the information is fast and accurate; sometimes it is slow and false. In both cases the system reacts. To be able to win it is essential that the company is aware of the feedback loops, understands and 'reads' them and takes appropriate proactive action rather than just letting the system do the reacting.

7

Be flexible and fast

With the arrival of strategic and long-term planning some decades ago, the decision-making process took one step backwards. It became fashionable to take decisions as soon as possible so that the company could implement the decisions as diligently and with as much planning as possible. This led to rigidity and lack of ability to accept and use change.

We had a situation where the planning horizon was lengthened so that media budgets were set for a 12-month period, promotional programmes were settled by calendar year and product launches were planned in detail one or even two years ahead of the launch. Many operations still follow this way of working and are, as a rule, not particularly successful.

Flexibility

While the decision-making and the implementation processes in most cases gain from being well established and set up, the decisions regarding *what* to do should be taken as late as possible. The later the decision is made, the more information will be available as to what is going on in the marketplace and the less chance that something will change between the time of the decision and its implementation in the marketplace.

EXAMPLE 7.1

The difference between 'how' and 'what' was highlighted in a sequence of events between a supplying company and one of the leading retailing organizations in the UK, J Sainsbury's. The issue at stake was a promotion. The way promotions are decided at Sainsbury's is, of course, a well-established routine and in this case a tentative agreement was reached in November for a promotion at the end of January. The final offer regarding terms for the promotion was negotiated on a Tuesday in mid-January, it was accepted and decided upon by the Sainsbury's price committee on the Thursday and the first orders of the promotional stock were placed the following week.

The crucial pricing issue was settled as late as possible while the principles were agreed well in advance, and the procedure for dealing with this element of the marketing mix had been in place for months or even years.

Observing executives in various capacities, it has often struck me that many very successful managers are terrible procrastinators and do not make decisions until the very last moment. While this is extremely frustrating for those who are kept waiting, it does actually mean, everything else being equal, that the decisions are of a better quality.

This type of behaviour can be perceived as being slow while, in reality, it is quite the reverse. By waiting until the last minute, the implementation has to be fast and the decision as such is made with the maximum amount of flexibility as any decision can be changed prior to its actual announcement.

A more turbulent marketplace requires more alternatives to possible decisions. If the environment is under greater stress and change, there are more possible solutions to consider to a problem or an opportunity. While in the past it might have been sufficient to review two or three different positioning concepts for a product, in a dynamic and changing world it might require 40!

From an organizational point of view, a decision-making process that is built around procedures and flexibility requires a 'flat' structure. The fewer layers there are between the top decision makers and the implementation level, the quicker it will happen. Over the last years delayering and destaffing have become popular buzz-words, and despite the fad element in management theories a flatter organization is usually more apt for dealing with fast decision-making.

Many aspects of chaos marketing require flexibility not only in action but also in mixing apparently contradictory strategies. It is necessary to have a long-term view but only if it is based on short term successes. Routines, which are systematic and usually blamed for causing people to think in rigid terms, need to be in place so that the executives can improvise and be flexible. The 'how to do' decisions are based on bureaucracy and systems but the 'what to do' decisions should be made as late as possible and with as many alternatives reviewed as possible.

Speed in implementation

The necessity for sharp action requires a mix of the long horizon with the short, and of being systematic while at the same time having the ability to improvise.

In order to be able to react quickly a company needs to be fast on its feet. The reaction time needs to be as short as possible. If each decision is based on reviewing an issue from scratch and setting up a way of dealing with it, fast footwork becomes an impossibility. The 'architecture', the structure, needs to be in place so that information is available and decisions can be executed quickly. Please note that the word 'structure' is used in a symbolic sense. Structure in this context is the same as a clear awareness and understanding among the employees of *how* to do things and a common understanding of company strengths, philosophy and objectives.

EXAMPLE 7.2

Advertising is a craft that often works with fairly long lead times. To do a television commercial usually takes six months from start to finish; a press advertisement might take at least a couple of months.

In December 1992 I visited Colin Glass, the then marketing director of Dixon's, the leading UK electrical goods retailer. In his office, in a corner, was a fax machine and as we entered at around noon the machine was busy churning out copies of that morning's competitive advertising. Later that afternoon, the marketing director and his advertising agency would agree on a revision to the Dixon's advertisement for the following day and by 6 p.m. a new advertisement was on its way to the press for publication the following morning.

Such quick action was possible because there was a procedure in place to deal with the required action. At Christmas, the most important time of the year for electrical goods, the important decisions were related to the goods that should be featured and at what price. The feedback for that decision was only available the day before the advertisement was to appear. The necessary data for the decision (profitability, availability, etc.) was prepared beforehand as well as the systems to deal with the alternative executions and routines.

With improvement in communication systems, offers that once could be deliberated over for quite some time, today need to be picked up very quickly as they otherwise will go to other players in the market. Also, this increases the possibilities of stopping a negative trend at the early stages. Provided that the feedback system is sufficiently sensitive to pick up negative issues, a fast-reacting system will quickly provide management with information to allow a fast decision whether to take action and, if so, what to do. If action is to be taken it is usually so that early action will require less resources to achieve the objectives.

Ensuring that the systems are in place and that everyone is aware of what is going on and where the company is going requires a long-term perspective. Short-term measures do not build the necessary architecture. When the marketplace is rocking backwards and forwards and competitors are taking all kinds of actions, the long-term view is a necessary target for the actions that need to be taken. At the same time, it is a well-proved management principle that without survival in the short term, there is no long term.

To summarize, all actions should be justifiable in the short term while the objectives should always be based on a long-term view. For similar reasons it is essential to be systematic when looking at the marketplace and putting routines in place, as otherwise the company will suboptimize its resources and it is only with the help of a systematic approach and routines that a company will have the ability to improvise without distracting from the on-going business.

To deal with change in the short term, managers need to be flexible and have the ability and inclination to improvise. With the structure in place that becomes easier as the routine issues will be dealt with 'anyway' provided that the routines have not led to complacency and lack of will to adapt and change.

Summary

If a company is to prosper in a turbulent marketplace it needs to be aware of the necessity of fast decisions and flexibility in the management structure. Procedures need to be in place to deal with the unknown and decisions should be made as late as possible to minimize the uncertainties.

8

Decrease the risks

Even if we recognize that the business world is becoming increasingly turbulent, we still need to plan our business and in order to get the best out of our investments in time and money we like to reduce the uncertainties.

What we do know is that what we plan will never materialize exactly as we planned it, but if we take certain precautions and follow a few rules, such as understanding the concepts of non-repetitive repetitiveness and boundaries, the probability of our plans being successfully implemented will increase.

Probabilities play an important role in the conceptual thinking of a chaos marketing executive. We have to allow for things to go wrong and we have to have an understanding of the degree to which the marketing mix dimensions will vary. It is also essential to remember the important lesson from chaos theory: i.e. even if we continually repeat one type of activity the result will not converge to an average. The environment is changing constantly, so even though our actions are the same, the result will not repeat itself, but will only resemble the results of the previous activities. However, the tighter we can define the boundaries and the more we can reduce the uncertainties within the marketing mix functions, the more predictable the outcome will be.

There are three ways of decreasing the risk in this context:

- increase market knowledge
- accumulate experience
- aim for perfection.

Increase market knowledge

The more knowledge executives have of a certain market sector, the more likely it is that the actions taken will be correct.

The market know-how can be in the form of either formal feedback, such as statistics, market research reports, etc., or informal feedback, such as qualitative knowledge built up over time in the business sector.

Knowledge of a market sector is not only about knowing the brand shares and the latest sales figures. To be successful one also needs to understand why that market and its sales have developed; and the reasons for the growth or decline or for the rejection or assimilation of new ideas. Thorough market knowledge is invaluable as it allows the executives to make better decisions, and because they have that knowledge they can judge and take action much more quickly, outpacing their rivals.

EXAMPLE 8.1

In the general rush to launch various cellular phone systems in the UK in the 1980s, several different systems were launched. The most original and unusual was 'Rabbit'.

Rabbit was in a sense a quite ingenious type of mobile phone as it used a much cheaper system to link the individual units to the telephone network. Rather than the expensive cellular base station system used by the 'traditional' mobile phone systems, such as Vodaphone and Cellnet, Rabbit relied on 'phone points', small boxes on, for instance, a wall, acting as receivers and located mainly in the London area. You could use the Rabbit telephone when you were within 1–200 metres of one of these 12 000 Rabbit phone points.

The system had two main advantages and two main disadvantages. The advantages were that it was a significantly cheaper system to use than ordinary cellular phones and it did use digital technology which meant that the signal quality was superior to the regular mobile phones at the time. The disadvantages were that you could only make outgoing calls with the Rabbit phone, not receive any, and the phones would only work near a phone point which restricted the areas in which it could be used.

The system was closed down in 1993 as 'the Rabbit telepoint service was not suitable for ... the UK market' (*Marketing* magazine, January 1994).

Rabbit did not suit the urban situation in London; the technical limitations were a drawback and despite high awareness the system was not a success. Better knowledge of the potential customers and willingness to understand the marketplace could have saved an expensive launch.

The other part of the market system is the internal, in-company, situation. Company knowledge is an integral part of achieving a clear understanding of the marketplace. The capabilities of the organization, the ability to respond, the internal strengths and weaknesses are all factors influencing the market system and represent necessary information in order to be able to maximize the company's presence in the market.

A marketing executive will never learn all there is to learn as the environment is in constant evolution. That, however, is not an excuse for not learning as much as possible. In order to minimize risks and maximize the potential, thorough market know-how is an essential ingredient.

Accumulate experience

It makes obvious logical sense to assume that the more you know about a market sector, and the more experience you have, the better your ability to judge the consequences of certain actions— understanding the non-repetitive repetitiveness. To draw a parallel with the medical sector, a doctor with several years' experience will be more likely to diagnose a disease correctly than someone straight from medical school.

A marketplace is a complex system and it takes time to understand fully how it is likely to react to various stimuli in the form of new products and communication. It is important to note, however, that it is not the years of service that count but the amount of relevant experience and the ability to put that experience to use.

EXAMPLE 8.2

In recent years one of the most successful frozen food companies in the United States is Luigino's Inc. The company was founded in the autumn of 1990 and by the end of 1993 already had an annual turnover of around $250 million in frozen prepared meals, a market sector that is neither high-tech nor flush with promotional resources.

One of the key reasons for the fast growth was that although the company was new, members of the initial team had over 700 years of experience between them. The founder and owner of the company, Mr Jeno Paulucci, had been in the food business since 1944 and the rest of the team had worked with him in several earlier successful ventures.

The advantage of experienced personnel is that they make fewer mistakes because they have a greater ability to judge whether or not something will work—assuming that the individuals continue to learn and accumulate up-to-date information.

Aim for perfection

In some literature on management in a chaotic world, it is advocated that it is better to throw a lot of products into the marketplace and see what happens rather than first perfect the product within the company. Experience does not support that view, and neither does the theory.

Such a strategy is unworkable for a supplying company dealing with and dependent on distribution channels outside its direct control. The wholesaler, distributor or retailer is unlikely to accept that its operation is 'clogged' with a number of new products, few of which will have a chance of succeeding.

In the case of a company controlling the total chain, such as Marks & Spencer's in the food and clothes markets, the situation is different. It is possible to try a number of new ideas and record what is happening, which is exactly what M&S has done with their chilled prepared meals range over the last decade. But unless in each case the product is as close to perfection as possible, it will still be a waste of resources. The M&S approach to product development reflects this; each product is reviewed and looked at in minute detail before it is permitted to be produced and featured in store.

The Japanese philosophy during the 1980s to launch a great number of variants of a product as quickly as possible has often been quoted as a reason for Western companies to do likewise. There are two important points to bear in mind in this context.

1 The Japanese companies had a deliberate management strategy to learn from each case, and that knowledge was immediately recycled into the company. In other words, they were still aiming for perfection but from a different angle than the traditional Western approach of extensive market research.
2 Most Japanese companies came to realize by the end of the decade that the strategy was not successful and started to prune the product ranges in order to be able to focus on the main profit generators rather than having a vast product portfolio—the latter being the result of a too-frivolous approach to launching new products and product variations. For instance, the large Japanese food group Ajinomoto decided to cut its range in half to 2500 items after realizing that 40 per cent of the product lines contributed only 3 per cent of sales.

Each marketing plan consists of a number of activities, each designed to cause a certain effect. The more exactly these activities are executed, the better the total result as the probabilities of mistakes have been reduced. By executing all functions and dimensions of a product and the promotional support to the highest possible standard within the given cost parameters, the marketer will ensure that his or her product will have the best chance of success. Successful products are almost without exception built on executional superiority: Coca-Cola, Kodak, Volkswagen, etc., all represent quality products.

It is worth noting, however, the old marketing truth that 'it does not help to produce a superior mouse trap if you do not tell the world about it'. Quality in itself does not sell and the product-idea graveyard is full of examples of excellent products that did not succeed; but that is not an excuse for not aiming for product superiority.

Attention to detail does mean that the risk of failure is minimized, the variance within which the system can move is reduced, and the chances for sustainable success are enhanced.

Summary

All of our actions in the marketplace will result in some reaction among customers or competitors. A noteworthy conclusion is that we do not know exactly what the outcome will be, we can only assume what will happen. As we are dealing with probabilities, in order to maximize the effects of our activities, it is essential that we also minimize the uncertainties and thus increase the probabilities of success.

To do this the marketing executives need to have extensive and up-to-date knowledge of the marketplace and the company's resources and capabilities; the individuals in charge must have marketing experience from the particular industry; and everybody involved should be aiming for perfection.

Mr Archie Norman, chief executive of the retailer ASDA, said in an interview: 'Everything you do has to be integrated. It is the small moves integrated across the business that make things happen.'

9

Reduce volatility

In Chapter 5 it was explained how a brand leading company can benefit from greater stability. Although a dynamic environment is always to be preferred to a stagnant one, as a rule it is in the interest of a leading company that the pace of change is relatively slow and definitely not volatile.

From that perspective it is of value to explore the ways in which a company might be able to stabilize the market system. How can a company increase the possibilities of operating in a non-volatile marketplace? From a defensive point of view it is a question of keeping the stabilizing dimensions in force, and from an offensive point of view the issue is to investigate whether it is possible to change the marketing mix so that greater emphasis can be put on the non-volatile dimensions and, in so doing, ensure that the company continues to dominate the market.

Recognize the stabilizing dimensions

The first step in a proactive strategy to move the rate of change in a direction that is most favourable to the company, is to recognize those factors that are stabilizing the market system in question and discover how the company can influence those factors or dimensions. The main stabilizing dimensions are distribution, communication and personal selling.

In most market situations the best opportunity for keeping a market stable is to focus on distribution and availability. The availability is a key element in any marketing mix. The importance of distribution is obvious in that if the product cannot reach its potential customers, everything else becomes insignificant.

The distribution systems are such a powerful part of the marketing mix as they link the various parts (subsystems) together through the physical activity of shipping products. If the supplying company can control the link, the customers' ability to change decreases as they are effectively without choice and the total system becomes more stable. The importance of this aspect is also illustrated by the fact that most companies entering a market adapt to the prevailing distribution systems.

The distribution system is often one of the largest cost elements when looking at the total costs for a product from raw material sourcing to ultimate use. It is not unusual that the distribution costs, in total, represent one-third of what the end user pays. There is also an element of significant scale effects: the big operators have a distinct advantage as you need a volume base to be able to run a distribution network. From a marketing point of view the distribution element can be as important as primary production for achieving an attractive value-for-money offer.

The fact that distribution systems are so expensive to run has meant that many companies have made accountant-led decisions to change, rather than look at, the marketing implications. A strong position based on distribution strengths has been abandoned as it was perceived in the short term that it was too expensive to run.

EXAMPLE 9.1

The frozen food and ice-cream industries are interesting examples of the power of the availability dimension.

Twenty to 30 years ago shops could only get frozen foods from a frozen food manufacturer. In the UK this meant that you either bought from Bird's Eye (Unilever), Ross or Findus. These three companies dominated the market as they controlled the distribution.

This situation changed, particularly during the late 1970s and 1980s, and today none of these three companies has its own distribution system. In each case, and especially for Bird's Eye and Findus, the brand share has fallen dramatically.

The pattern is different for ice cream. Historically the situation was the same: you could only get ice cream from Wall's (Unilever) or Lyons-Maid. The difference to frozen foods is that today Wall's ice cream is still, to a significant degree, being distributed on Unilever-'controlled' wheels. The situation for Lyons-Maid has developed in a different way for other reasons, so I shall omit that from the scenario.

While the distribution of ice cream, not only in the UK but also in the rest of Europe, has remained in the hands of the manufacturers and/or brands, companies in this market sector have in most cases an above-average profit level. In addition, Wall's, with its continental sister companies, has been able to defend its market shares much more effectively than the 'sister' frozen food operations.

The launch of the Mars ice-cream bar in 1989–90 illustrates further the importance of controlling the availability dimension. In markets where Mars managed to get distribution effectively, such as the UK, the product made a significant impact. In markets where the distribution system was more difficult to break into, such as Germany, the success was much more limited. In addition, the practice in many markets of brand-controlled, and paid for, display freezers in some outlets meant that Mars faced further problems to reach all potential customers. Mars had either to abandon these opportunities or invest themselves in display freezers, the latter representing a significant investment. From the perspective of the existing brands, the availability factors had a significant stabilizing impact, in a positive sense, on the sales of existing brands when faced with the threat of a new competitor.

A similar example to ice cream is the previously mentioned link between the breweries and the pubs. By controlling the flow from barley to glass the breweries' market position has been insulated against change. The situation has changed recently due to new legislation, but much of the effects remain.

Fully integrated retailers also control the forward distribution of their products in that they have full control from the manufacturing of the goods to the display on the shelves. At least one uncertainty, whether a product will be listed by the retailer or not, is taken out of the system. A system with less uncertainty is of course less volatile.

The same situation seen from the perspective of a manufacturer can be extremely volatile in that only one decision, to list or not to list, can determine whether a product will be displayed or not. Once the product is on the shelves the probabilities change as the product and the company are dependent not on one decision maker but on hundreds of customers, and thus there is the probability for at least some sales increase.

From the above it is apparent that a business entity that controls the distribution to the ultimate customers is in an enviable position to use that tool to its advantage.

Another way of looking at the relationship between supplier and customer is to use the opportunity of savings one can generate by having a more effective supply chain to reduce stocks and lead times: 'partnership sourcing' is the term most commonly used. A secondary effect of such an arrangement is that the supplier–customer link strengthens.

These kinds of links are being set up all over the world. The leading companies in this respect were the Japanese auto manufacturers, such as Toyota, where close integration meant that lead times and, above all, stocks were reduced to a minimum. This is also happening in the FMCG business: for instance, Procter & Gamble in the US has a link up with Wal-Mart, one of its largest customers, so that when a product passes through the checkout it is immediately replaced. Another example involving DuPont, the US textile manufacturer, was quoted by Sir John Harvey-Jones in a magazine interview:

> DuPont makes the fibres, from that another company makes the yarn and cloth, from that another company makes children's clothes which then go to one of the major retail chains, and they are all sharing all their logistical information. Now they've cut their total costs by over a third.

By dominating a dimension that represents stability, such as distribution, companies have been able to keep a strong market position and keep a lot of change away from the market sector. If a rebel company cannot get distribution, it cannot influence the marketplace!

Distribution is not a stabilizing factor in all situations. Companies can innovate and create volatility by side-stepping the established channels. Most of these refer to operations starting to use direct mail in competition with the various traditional distribution systems. This has happened in the personal computer industry. The most famous example is Dell (see also Chapter 5); within a short period of time this company has managed to build a multi-million dollar business by by-passing the traditional distribution systems. With a changing marketplace the traditional distribution systems, dominated by IBM, did not change sufficiently quickly and did not adapt to the changing supply and demand situation, so Dell and its followers destabilized further a system that was once quite stable.

The availability dimension has been used above as an *example* of a stabilizing dimension because it is, subjectively, often underrated and can be a most powerful tool. Each market sector has one or several dimensions that act in a stabilizing way. To manage successfully it is important to realize that these dimensions exist so that the company can use them proactively to gain competitive advantages.

If a company is dominating the stabilizing dimensions, then it is essential for its future strategy that it takes actions to keep its position in these dimensions and to maintain their importance. In case the force of change is so strong that the existing stabilizing factors are likely to decline in importance, action should be taken to build up a new dimension of stability in order to maintain market positions.

Defuse volatility

If a market sector does not have a strong stabilizing factor, like distribution in the paragraphs above, what can a company do to avoid getting into a volatile and uncontrollable situation?

One route is to build a strong position in a potentially stabilizing dimension and by doing so increase the importance of that dimension to the marketing mix.

For a large company, advertising is usually the main alternative. For a smaller company dominating a small market segment, personal selling can be a more attractive alternative.

Advertising can stabilize a market system in two different ways. First, because of the scale effects of all media advertising and in particular television advertising, a large media budget creates a barrier to entry. It is very difficult and costly for a small brand to take on the brand leader's advertising budget as the smaller brand has less revenue over which to spread the costs. Secondly, the brand loyalty that advertising often creates is in itself a stabilizing factor.

Both factors together will make the market system even less volatile, as not only will the increased loyalty be fuelled by advertising but by keeping the spending at a high level, rebel, destabilizing companies will be discouraged from entering. Also, by spending more the importance of advertising in the total marketing mix will further increase.

EXAMPLE 9.2

An interesting example of this is currently taking place in Italy; and whether or not it will succeed is, at the time of writing, still uncertain. This is also a follow-on from the previous example as it refers to frozen foods.

In Italy the leading frozen food brand is Findus, owned in Italy by Unilever and not Nestlé. Findus has 'always' been the brand leader, and until five or six years ago this situation was unassailable due to the distribution strengths of the company. Findus is calling on over 70 000 individual shops with its own vehicles, covering more than double the number of outlets the No. 2 brand reaches.

As with everywhere else, due to a changing retail environment, the market conditions have started to change. The rising number of hyper- and supermarkets has meant that you can now reach more consumers through fewer stores. Alternative distribution systems are appearing and you no longer need to call on 30 000 shops to get, for a medium/large brand, a sufficient level of distribution.

Since the end of the 1980s Findus has, in Italy, embarked on a strategy with a much increased media spend. It appears that Findus is managing to retain its high brand share with the help of the increased advertising budgets. What the longer term effects will be for the Unilever subsidiary remains to be seen.

Everywhere else in Europe, when the distribution advantage has disappeared the share has dropped significantly; yet in Italy the Findus share is still over 50 per cent of the total frozen food market!

Proactive management of stabilizing dimensions

The logic of using a stabilizing dimension, outlined above, can be taken one step further. While advertising as such is a stabilizing dimension, it is not a homogeneous dimension. We have television advertising as well as magazines, daily papers, trade press, direct mail and outdoor. Each of these factors can be looked at individually and one can look at ways of making one factor more important than another, thus ensuring that the brand dominates a specific type of media.

Nescafé, the very successful instant coffee brand, had, and still appears to have, a media policy of only being in media where it can take a significant share. By dominating, it also stabilizes; and by spending significant amounts, the importance of that media increases for the market sector.

If a market is moving into a volatile situation and the chaos element is increasing, one has to recognize that but it is not necessary to follow the trend. A strong brand can take action to build stability and thus counter the system's trend towards total instability. By selecting dimensions that will stabilize, the marketer has the opportunity to defuse volatility.

The interaction between different parts of the market system and the marketing mix does open up the possibilities of defusing volatility, not by countering activities where they are happening but by activating other elements of the marketing mix. Like Findus Italy, when the power of distribution is likely to disappear, extra investments are made in advertising.

The proactive marketer has also the advantage of being the one 'choosing the weapons'. The company or brand that takes the initiative will influence how the competitive battle will be fought. If a company has certain skills—for instance, in direct communication or personal selling—these activities can be fielded actively and thus set the scene for, potentially, challenging companies.

Consumer goods vs industrial goods

It appears by looking at the total marketplace that consumer goods brands systems are more stable than those of industrial goods. Consumer brands are old; the average age of the top 20 brands in the UK grocery trade is over 50 years, and many of the companies behind these brands are long established.

The main reason for consumer brands, and companies, 'staying alive' longer is that there is a greater emphasis on communication and on brand building in general. These factors contribute to a more stable environment.

An additional effect is caused by the relative low input of novel technology in many consumer goods products. Despite the influx of home electronics, the majority of household goods are traditional in construction and usage: in other words, one volatile dimension, innovation, is less predominant.

Brand-leading industrial goods suppliers have here a golden opportunity to take the initiative and replicate the principles behind the FMCG companies' long-term strengths. While it is true that the FMCG tactics are not generally applicable, the strategies are. Taking a less orthodox view on marketing strategy, industrial goods companies can build less volatile market systems. By focusing on more stabilizing factors and ensuring that the systems are not allowed to get out of control, they can, in contrast to companies such as IBM, strengthen their long-term possibilities. There are analytically no predetermined reasons for industrial goods markets to act in a more volatile way than consumer goods markets.

Finally, services are no different from products. Greater stability can be created by strengthening chosen factors such as distribution, i.e. making the service easily available, and different types of communication and personal selling.

Summary

This chapter illustrated how it is in principle possible to prepare for and, if necessary, defuse a volatile market development by using stabilizing marketing mix dimensions achieving a less dynamic chaos system. There are various techniques one can use; the outcome is never certain but the result is likely to be better than not doing anything at all or, even worse, to be forced to compete on the challenger's terms.

The purpose of exploring the various avenues is not to suggest single-mindedly that a brand leader should always try to stabilize the system and always work against volatility. It is only to suggest that there are ways of tackling volatility and preserving a 'proper' dynamic environment.

For companies that are in a situation where they possess a dimension that is strongly stabilizing a system in their favour, it is essential to develop this dimension so it will be possible to continue to bear the fruits of this in the future.

When a leading company is facing increasing volatility, and most companies do, it is not enough to be aware of change—as has been described earlier—but action must be taken to support the brand's status and build for the future.

10

Ride on the crest of chaos

One way of looking at marketing in a turbulent world is to
investigate and implement ways of 'coping' with and 'smoothing'
the chaos. As soon as there is something unknown, most executives
like to find ways to settle the situation and get it back to 'normal'. In
reality it is becoming more and more unlikely that situations will 'go
back' to normal, and so the abnormal becomes the normal.

Accepting this view of the world, one can set out on a strategy of
defusing the situation and that approach was described in the previous
chapter. For someone in a brand-leading position with a profitable
business that approach might very well be most appropriate.

The alternative strategy is to set out to create dynamic chaos. By
setting off events it is possible to change the marketing system, by
using guerrilla type tactics in order to unsettle the established
marketplace, a challenging company can create a competitive
advantage.

The advantages come in two different shapes. First, it is likely, but
not certain, that the newcomer is quicker to react and adapt to the
changes. Secondly, by being the initiator of the process, the
challenger has a head start in being aware of what is happening
before anyone else and can be properly prepared.

The one thing to bear in mind is a lesson from chaos theory: the
faster the process of change, the more difficult it will be to predict
the outcome. It is by no means certain that the change process will
develop as intended; indeed many companies have set in motion
processes that they later would have wished they had never started.

In most situations the objective of creating turbulence is to unsettle
a competitor or a marketplace where a company wishes to enter or
gain a much larger share. The technique can also be used in a
company's own marketing system; by creating a lot of change, the
parameters are altered and the position of the company is
transformed. Many have set off on such a strategy, intentionally or

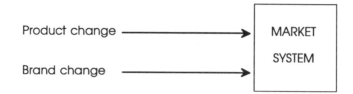

Figure 10.1 Creating chaos in the marketplace

unintentionally, only to wake up to the fact that they have lost
share, such as IBM in the personal computer market; but sometimes
the strategy does work, Guinness UK being one example.

In a situation where a company wishes to create chaos there are, in
principle, two steps. The first is to unsettle the system by increasing
the pace of change—for instance, bombarding the customers with
new products, new ways of doing business or perhaps totally new
messages. The second is to act so that the unstable system actually
moves in the intended direction by, for instance, communicating
certain messages, launching a specific type of product or pushing
the price level down by x per cent.

One can divide the various ways of creating chaos into those that
are product related and those that are tied to the brand and brand
image (Figure 10.1).

Product-generated chaos

There are many ways of creating chaos by changing the product
dimension; this is usually done by introducing something totally
new, or dramatically lowering the price base, or using a combination
of these two.

For the longer term a change based on a new product concept is
much more tenable than just a price cut to achieve higher sales
volume, which is why so much attention is being spent on finding
new concepts. It is, however, often a route that fails; only around 30
per cent of new FMCG products survive two years on the market
but when successful the changes can be most dramatic.

The company that sets the wheels in motion is not always the one
that reaps the benefits. This point can be illustrated by two
examples from the car industry during the 1960s and 1970s.

EXAMPLE 10.1

The Mini was the creation of Sir Alec Issigonis. From its first launch the
Mini made a dramatic impact; it was the first small car with status value,
it was fun to drive and it also featured a number of technical
innovations. For reasons that are perhaps best left out of this book, BMC,
BMCL and/or British Leyland never capitalized on this change to
establish itself firmly in the new sector it had created and lead. The
'new' type of motoring that the Mini introduced was exploited by
Renault, Volkswagen and many other manufacturers.

EXAMPLE 10.2

The Japanese car 'invasion' started in the mid/late 1960s. Initially the
basis for the change dynamics was very simple: a reliable car at a competitive price. This concept was not particularly unique, it was just that
the manufacturers, particularly in the US, had ignored the basic criteria
for cars, i.e. that they should represent value for money and be reliable.

However, the Japanese managed to exploit the change they had
created. By continually launching new products and by adding all kinds
of extras to them in combination with lean production (= low prices)
and a much faster turn around for new models, Toyota, Nissan, Honda,
etc., all rode on the crest of change and pushed their boundaries
forward. They certainly capitalized on the changes they set in motion.

The conclusion of these two examples is that if you are going to
change the pace and the direction of a market, you have to be
prepared to act in order to be able to reap the benefits. The whole
organization has to be geared up to deal with the new opportunities
and to be aware that these opportunities will not be pre-planned
and they will appear in an unpredictable way. This makes short lead
times, fast feedback loops and good understanding of the customers
essential ingredients for success.

For organizations that have built a business from product-generated
chaos, the future strategy becomes somewhat of a dilemma. One
strategy is to retain all the elements of the key ingredients required
for survival in such a market and continue to innovate. The problem
with such a strategy is that the opportunities to change the systems
might well diminish as the technology-led dimensions perhaps no
longer are as attractive. The customers might even begin to
appreciate totally different dimensions, such as being negative
rather than positive to change.

Another strategy is to move into a stabilizing mode and build
dimensions that fulfil such a strategy: brand building, intangible
benefits etc. Such a strategy requires a change in corporate
philosophy and that the company involved builds up a new and

different type of competence. Toyota and Nissan, for instance, have chosen this strategy.

The totally product-related approach described above is a fairly long-term activity in that it entails product development and other core competences. A more short-term and quick way of creating turbulence is to reduce the price dramatically. Although it is a strategy that is fairly easy to implement, the consequences might be as significant as those outlined and illustrated previously.

The main concern to bear in mind is that unless the strategy is built on solid cost advantages it can be a most dangerous way of attempting to build business. It is almost certain that the competition will respond similarly, and the only effect might be that customer behaviour becomes even more unpredictable. It is by no means certain that any additional sales volume will offset the loss in margins.

Most of today's increased turbulence is fuelled by information technology. In recent years one of the most significant changes has been the dramatic rise of the computer games industry. The simple pocket computer game that saw the light of day in the very early 1980s has moved forward at a rapid pace with all kinds of technological innovations. The industry to which the games belong is even questionable: are they part of the toy industry, or entertainment, or leisure, or home electronics? For the customers such definitions do not matter and it is quite significant that a market in rapid change is one that is difficult to pinpoint to a specific part of the existing market structure.

EXAMPLE 10.3

The worldwide computer market for 1993 is estimated to be worth £9 billion, with sales of £750 million in Britain alone. It is also estimated that in Britain one household in three has a computer game console of some sort. To further illustrate the impact of this new concept, it has been reported that in 1993 British children spent more on Nintendo games alone than records, CDs and videos, and in the US Nintendo had revenues in excess of all the Hollywood studios and more than the three national TV networks together. This market sector has been created in approximately 10 years.

The two main companies in this market, SEGA and Nintendo, have created change by launching and developing increasingly attractive and sophisticated games. It is also significant for the nature of a market in rapid change that the company that set off the market sector in the first place, Atari, is now far behind the major companies due to a misjudged product development programme.

This market is not only about products but also about communication. In addition to product innovation, SEGA and Nintendo are fuelling change by their marketing programmes and as such providing illustrations of how 'change marketing' can be used. The marketing strategies of both companies aim for building stability with the target audience, while at the same time driving the instability of the market, changing the traditional way of marketing.

SEGA's European marketing director has described this as 'pirating marketing conventions', using the traditional tools but in an unorthodox way. SEGA uses television advertising in the traditional way but the creative execution is unusual. The brand launched its own SEGA TV with the message that this TV station has hijacked the airwaves and subverts normal advertisements, 'gentle anarchy' according to the advertising agency involved. Not only is the creative content anarchic, the placement is done with a lot of consideration for building 'street credibility'. A traditional media schedule would favour pop shows and teenage chat shows, but such a schedule would be boring and predictable. A sharp and dynamic commercial has much greater 'turbulence' value in a family programme such as 'Blind Date'. By putting the advertisement in that environment, credibility is gained by going against the system. The brand also went into football sponsoring in a new way and in doing so virtually hijacked the broadcasting of the European Championships.

The communication of turbulence is balanced by techniques to build links with the target group to stabilize the relationships. Strong links and feedback loops are built with the audience by programmes such as a sales promotion activity giving school children the opportunity to write their own marketing plan and then taking the winners on to a SEGA Advisory Board.

Nintendo has a club which all purchasers join automatically. With the club the users get information about the games, special offers and also access to a 24-hour help line. All are classic techniques for building loyalty through linkage and also allows Nintendo to get feedback quickly regarding the views of a target group with very fickle habits.

Communication-generated chaos

The above example illustrates not only what one can do with product innovation but, in particular, how the communication programme can be used to find an apparently chaotic approach while in reality aiming for the 'classic' stabilizing effects of brand loyalty.

In order to set in motion changes in the true sense of the word, the aggressive challenger has to look in other directions. From a communication point of view there are three different ways chaos can be induced:

- by hijacking someone else's brand property
- by communicating in ways that are truly considered out-of-bounds by the target group
- by choosing messages that are totally unexpected.

The first of these techniques, hijacking someone else's brand property and using it to boost the company's own brand, is a fairly new phenomenon, mainly used outside Europe and in particular in the United States.

The technique is simply to use another brand's reputation to establish one's own brand. Provided the communication is created in the 'right' way, the challenger will pinch the brand leader's reputation through a 'rub-off' effect of some key value dimensions. The most well-known case is Pepsi's use of comparative advertising versus Coca-Cola. By placing the Coca-Cola brand on parity with Pepsi (or slightly behind) the market hierarchy was disturbed. When the advertising campaign started, Pepsi was a much smaller brand than Coca-Cola. That is no longer the case. This strategy puts the leader in a difficult situation because if the company responds in the same way, the credibility for the challenger will increase even more. Needless to say, the best strategy for a brand leader is to ensure that its products are so good that it is not possible for a challenger to run successful comparative advertising campaigns. (See also Chapter 17.)

A secondary effect of comparative advertising is that it moves the focus of the communication away from emotional, intangible, dimensions to product features—a potentially more volatile part of the value mix. If the comparison is featuring a new product this effect can be even more pronounced.

As with most destabilizing strategies, this one will only be successful in the medium to long term if the challenger has an organization that is capable of exploiting the instability and gain in other aspects 'on the back of it', such as in the case of Pepsi broadening its distribution base.

The second strategy is the communication equivalent of launching a dramatically new product. When a totally new advertising campaign breaks and the creative values are such that the target groups react with total amazement, then it is a destabilizing campaign.

The most well-known and talked about attempt to do just that is the Benetton advertising of recent years. The posters with striking pictures—several of which were banned in the UK by the Advertising Standards Authority—created total amazement and new reactions to the Benetton brand.

While it is quite clear that the campaign did change the communication system between Benetton and its customers, it is not clear how it affected customer behaviour. This is not unusual for a chaos system; if you take unexpected turns, as Benetton did, you have to expect the unexpected, one possibility being that the customers may not react at all!

A more uncontroversial but still very creative approach is the Britvic Tango advertisements.

EXAMPLE 10.4

In 1991–92 Tango, a fizzy orange drink, started to feature in a series of rather bizarre commercials. Initially four commercials were created featuring an orange genie, an exploding granny, a jellyhanded 'Napoleon' and a strange man on the platform of a railway station. The characters crept upon people and shocked them in a variety of ways with the phrase 'Have you been Tango'd?'. The aim of the advertisements was to express Tango's 'extra orangey hit'.

The commercials created a lot of attention and the campaign was commercially successful. According to magazine reports sales increased by almost 30 per cent during the first 12 months of the campaign.

The third strategy is the traditional marketing executive's version of the second one. The campaign is unexpected but it is based on logic and a perceived opportunity in the marketplace. We have seen several attempts to achieve this, by a clever piece of communication shifting the market to play on the challenger's rules.

One classic example was the Volkswagen launch advertising in the United States. With headlines such as 'The car that the man who drives the snow plow drives' and 'Think small' Volkswagen changed the way a significant segment of the market would view a car purchase, moving it away from the chrome and the oversized engines to utility and practicality. The effect of the campaign was not only that it established the Volkswagen Beetle on the US market, an achievement in itself for this ugly but practical car, but that it changed the way cars were advertised—something that later was to be used by other European brands such as Volvo.

This strategy is a much safer option than the previous one but it does demand excellent creative quality. Other areas where this strategy has worked with some success is lager beer advertising in the UK. Heineken, Carling Black Label and, previously, Hofmeister have all moved their advertising into the field of humour, far away from the traditional beer advertising still prevalent in most parts of Europe.

EXAMPLE 10.5

An example of how a company totally changed the communication, without product change, to destabilize its own marketing system in order to get out of a declining spiral, is Guinness during the 1980s.

At the time of the great change of communication strategy in the mid-1980s Guinness was a very well respected brand, with classic advertising executed by the J. Walter Thompson advertising agency. The commercials almost oozed strong brand values, heritage, tradition, excellent taste, etc. What the commercials did not do was sell products. The communication was seen as old-fashioned and irrelevant for the key target group for any beer product, 18–25 year olds.

The first step in the revolution was the 'Guinnless' campaign, in its day probably as confusing for the over-30s as the SEGA campaign is today for the same age group. This was followed in 1988 by the 'Pure genius' campaign, with a message and visuals that were quite avant-garde.

The effect was increased sales for the first time 'in living memory' and for the first time Guinness became fashionable. The decision to go with the new communication programme was very brave as it broke all prevailing rules and the outcome was by no means certain. The communication programme did not really change the marketplace as a totality; nor did it force the rest of the beer market into change—probably at least partly due to the very strong stabilizing forces in that system—but it did change Guinness's own system, fortunately for the brand, in the 'right' direction. Sales increased by 30 per cent from 1988 to 1994 and in early 1994 Guinness reached its highest share ever of the total beer trade in the UK.

The Guinness example is really a mix of strategies two and three. It shows what one can do if the talent, money and market awareness are in place.

Summary

Creating turbulence and throwing markets off course is a technique that marketers rarely consider as it goes against the traditional way of working. Such a strategy carries a high risk. It is impossible to predict the outcome so it is essential to have as many feedback loops in place as possible and, in general, to keep the 'ears to the ground' so that corrective or exploitative action can be taken as soon as the opportunities arise. The Mini did not create a fortune for the British car industry, while the Japanese car manufacturers have had many years of very positive development. Whether SEGA and/or Nintendo will reap the benefits of their activities is too early to judge at the time of writing, but what is certain is that Volkswagen and Guinness did make a lot of money out of riding the crest of chaos.

PART FOUR

THE APPLICATION OF CHAOS MARKETING

The previous chapters have covered the thinking and theory behind successful marketing management in a turbulent world. It is of course essential to have a clear understanding of *why* certain actions need to be taken, but it is equally clear from the concept itself that one important part of the marketer's responsibilities is to ensure that action is taken, that the framework is used.

The following chapters will explain how 'chaos marketing' is best applied to the main parts of the marketing mix, covering the product-related issues as well as the promotion of the goods and/or services. I have deliberately focused on the main marketing tools to ensure that the concept will work where it is most relevant and will give best results.

11

Introduction

The importance of change

From an application point of view the marketer needs to pay
particular attention to:

- develop and enhance continuously
- keep the initiative
- take actions quickly
- have knowledge and stay involved.

All markets develop, some faster than others, and to ensure that one
does not lose any competitive advantages continuous change and
development are essential. It is not only the competitive situation
which triggers change, customers' views and circumstances change
as well; some of these changes one can predict, others will just
happen. For instance, according to the Henley Centre in the UK,
people's perception of high price as an indicator of high quality in
the cosmetics market changed from 35 per cent in 1985 to 54 per
cent in 1989 to 31 per cent in 1993. The successful marketer will
not only follow these trends but he or she will also influence the
rate of change by marketing actions.

All experience of the last decades point clearly to the conclusion
that change is necessary. The old saying 'if it ain't broke, don't fix it'
is no longer applicable, if it ever was. To be successful one needs
continuously to enhance the competitive standing of the product or
service and even if 'it ain't broke' it will still need to be made
stronger.

The previous chapter, on the strategic alternatives in creating
change, highlighted the importance of keeping the initiative. The
brand that sets the agenda is also the one that is most likely to get a
marketing mix battle on the 'most favourable terms'.

The most successful market entries have taken place in areas where the leading brands have become complacent and inactive, continuing along a furrow that was ploughed a long time ago. Striking examples of this are the US automobile and the British motorcycle industries of the 1960s and 1970s. The Japanese appeared and offered products that were perceived as better value for money and changed the competitive scene, in the case of cars from glitz and big to reliability and price. Similarly, in the consumer electronics field, the Japanese companies with innovation upon innovation (not invention) totally unsettled the Western companies.

Another more recent example of the dangers of losing the initiative is IBM and the personal computer market. Although IBM is credited with creating the PC concept in the first place they did not keep the initiative and the market was taken away from IBM by Apple, Compaq, Dell, etc.

These examples can be contrasted by some of the leading FMCG brands in Britain. By taking the initiative in the field of product enhancement and consumer communication, Nescafé has managed over the last 15 years to fight off attacks from private labels, cheap-branded imports as well as other domestic-branded competitors. The new entrants have not been able to get a response for innovations, such as the Unilever Red Mountain instant coffee mix with ground coffee granules, nor have they managed with lower prices to gain share from Nescafé. Large and effective advertising campaigns and product enhancement have maintained consumer (and retail trade) loyalty.

The third aspect to bear in mind as a marketer is that action needs to be taken quickly. Fast implementation is becoming a necessity. Modern electronics and, in particular, communication methods have made it a necessity to be as fast as the media. It is unlikely that someone will get a competitive advantage just out of being fast, but it is most likely that a company that is slow will be at a competitive disadvantage. The difference between the changing pace of communication and the changing habits is an important element in this scenario. Many habits change very slowly and others quite quickly, but the communication of whatever change there is will continue to flow faster and faster.

The fourth point from above, knowledge and involvement, refers to the key personal commitment that is required from someone who is to succeed. Experience and knowledge will become increasingly important in a company's quest for faster implementation as it is much more likely that knowledgeable executives will be able to do the 'right thing' faster than someone who is new to a business.

While knowledge is all about understanding a business, involvement will generate a total understanding. Successful executives are always involved, knowing the details of the industry, understanding the customers, taking a 24-hour interest in what is going on.

Summary

The points above serve as an introduction to the following chapters. In a turbulent world the simple rules outlined above are of paramount importance; it is important to understand what to do, and it is essential to know how to do it, but knowledge without actions become only hallucinations.

12

Range management

One of the main parts of the marketer's responsibility is to ensure that the product range for which he or she is responsible is managed and developed in the best possible way. There are many aspects to range management and in this chapter I shall focus on how to classify the various products within a range in order to best apply the chaos concept and what the consequences are of the classification. My concerns in this chapter refer totally to those products a company already has on the market, not any new developments. These are covered in the following chapter.

To categorize the various types of products within a range I shall use the three expressions: builders, parasites and wobblers. The definition of each will soon become apparent but for a short definition: a *builder* is a product that is at the core of the range and company, solid and with a large sales volume; a *parasite* is a slow seller with a limited market appeal; and a *wobbler* is a product that potentially could 'wobble' into being a 'builder' or a 'parasite'.

Range management has been of universal importance for a long time. The subject is creating greater interest in the context of a dynamic marketplace as with a greater degree of real and perceived change and the pitfalls that this brings with it, it becomes even more essential than before to constantly reassess the product portfolio. To do that clear and manageable concepts can be very useful.

A particular consequence is that the opportunities to turn a wobbler into a builder will come about at an increasingly higher speed and the chaos techniques of creating feedback loops and 'nudging' products in a specific direction will make range management an even more exciting subject than in the past.

Range analysis

Computers have made the traditional range analysis of ranking products according to sales, marginal contribution, net profits, etc., in relative and absolute terms a task that can be performed in seconds rather than days. Although this type of data is essential to define the builders and the parasites, it will only provide part of the picture.

Looking at the total supply chain for the product to reach the customers, in most cases each company is only responsible for one part of the chain. Upstream there are suppliers and downstream customers for further processing or sales. Even in the consumer goods industry it is not necessarily the retailer who is the final seller; the individual buying a product in a supermarket is often not the user and needs to 'sell' the purchase to the 'customers' at home.

A holistic view of the supply chain and the financial dimensions within it can make the traditional range analysis look 'narrow-minded'. In most instances the profitability of a product is based on the manufacturing costs, but in a developed market that is often only a small part of the total cost. Distribution and/or selling expenses can be just as important, and, again, taking an FMCG product as an example, the largest cost element for a 'normal' supermarket product is often not the raw materials but the retailing cost, i.e. the cost of having a product on the shelf.

Reviewing the total cost picture can give a different perspective on the potential for a product, and broaden the horizon for a profitable development or discontinuation.

Understanding the total profitability picture is always important, but when the world is rapidly changing it becomes essential. The marketer often has the opportunity to influence the factors outside his or her 'normal' control—upstream through buyers and downstream through salespersons. Using this opportunity to nudge the system in the right direction can make great changes and turn wobblers into builders, and even create a sustainable competitive advantage.

Builders

Builders add value to the company in all respects. Products defined as builders have high sales rates and satisfactory relative profitability, they generate significant revenues and profits and usually contribute to boosting the overall image of a company and a brand.

Great care needs to be taken to ensure that the builders remain such. 'Old Product Development' is the key to successful management of builders and constant rejuvenation and enhancement is certain to give great returns, as has been proved in many cases. Well-known brands such as the Volkswagen Golf and Kellogg's Corn Flakes have managed to retain their position by constant gradual change; not allowing challengers to set the agenda but setting the agenda themselves and thus maintaining a position of 'builder'.

Strategies that suggest that existing strong products should be 'milked', i.e. under-invested in, or replaced by new products, following the product life cycle theory (see next chapter), should be avoided. Strong products have gained their position because they offer an attractive perceived value. That confidence and market position is very valuable.

Brands and products that are builders need to be maintained to remain so, and it should be the top priority of all marketing executives to have that as their first priority. Investments in product development, sales promotion, advertising, etc., will almost without exception generate a better return if linked to an existing product and brand. On the other hand, a product or brand that is getting no support will not remain a builder for very long—the changes in the marketplace and the competition will take care of that. In particular, the opportunities by challengers to change the marketing mix emphasis by attacking the dynamic marketing system can have profound and quick, but negative, effects on an unsupported builder product.

The usage of products and how customers react to enhancement follow the same pattern. A survey by Leo Burnett Advertising Agency in Chicago published in *The Economist* confirmed what many senior marketing executives have always suspected: when advertising can be shown to increase sales of established brands, the main increase (in this case 70 per cent of it) comes from existing users. As most buyers rotate between different brands, a strong advertising message can improve the brand loyalty in terms of frequency of buying with a healthy sales increase as a result. An example quoted in *The Economist* article was advertising for Maxwell House coffee in the USA where, of a 69 per cent sales increase, less than one-fifth came from totally new customers.

Builders are the key products in any product portfolio, and the key to success with these products is to focus on existing, more or less frequent, users of the products. To remain a builder the marketers must ensure that the products are developed and enhanced in tangible as well as intangible aspects.

Parasites

Parasites are the opposite of builders, and all companies have parasites in their product portfolios! They are products that have failed to gain a reasonable sales level and are hindering the development of the sound parts of the business. They use valuable management and sales time, and are vampires on the corporate body, obstructing the flow in the market system.

These products have too low a sales level and/or too low relative profit to generate sufficient returns to warrant a place on the price list. What 'sufficient' means in this instance differs, of course, from industry to industry and even from company to company, but it is not unusual for 20–30 per cent of a company's range to be in the parasite category.

In the vast majority of cases the only action someone needs to take when a parasite is found is to 'bring out the axe' and chop the product or service off the sales list. Occasionally there is a lesson to be learned by looking at why the product was never successful, or there might be a part of the idea worth keeping for another project.

Although parasites are a drain on company resources, most companies can cope with having some parasites in the range on an on-going basis. Just as in the biological world, a few parasites will do little harm, but if there are too many the company will die. Parasites distract management attention and they take up valuable financial, sales and technical resources. Distinct pruning is the best remedy.

Wobblers

Wobblers are those products that are not performing well enough to be a builder and are not bad enough to be a parasite on the corporate body, but could swing either way.

To have potential for turning into a builder the product needs to have one of the following characteristics:

- good relative profitability
- good sales rate
- high sales in a specific market sector.

If none of these circumstances is at hand, the product is unlikely to be saved and might as well be considered a parasite without any further analysis or marketing effort.

On the other hand, if it is profitable and the sales rate is too low, action might yield positive results. Similarly, if the sales rate is satisfactory but the profitability is not, a more holistic view of the profit generation might throw up possibilities for renegotiating the sharing of profits across the supply chain, or it might even be possible to generate additional marketing funds internally. Finally, if the product is doing well in a specific sector but that market segment is too small, a potential exists perhaps to extend usage to another submarket or it might be worth holding out on the expectation that the niche will grow.

To save and transform a wobbler the marketer can use a number of different 'chaos' techniques such as nudging the product in the right direction, changing the marketing system by incurring change at a faster pace, or introducing an innovation that will give it a competitive advantage. Traditional marketing methods such as building distribution, creating a personality and employing creative sales promotion ideas are, of course, not to be forgotten.

The marketing system is in many cases very sensitive to change and if the marketer improves the feedback loops so that it becomes easier and quicker to monitor what is happening, fairly small and relatively inexpensive changes can create significant change.

EXAMPLE 12.1

The Findus French Bread Pizza range was launched in the UK in 1979. The launch was initially very successful and created a new segment of the pizza market. Unfortunately, in 1981 the sales started to decline and by 1984 the sales were at a level where the future of the concept was questioned.

The range was reformulated in 1985 as a 'last' attempt to save the product group from disappearing. The quality was improved and a new variety was launched. The sales graph stabilized and showed some signs of turning.

The product activities were followed by the creation of new TV advertising, on screen in 1986. The new creative platform presented French Bread Pizza as a 'fun' product, the new commercial was very well received, and sales increased.

By 1988 sales had more than doubled from the level in 1984. The positive development generated more success as the 'normal' sales increase provided a basis for wider in-store distribution and also a few line extensions. The programme of improving the quality and new advertising changed a product group from being a candidate for parasite status in 1983–84 to a builder with a strong position in the market in 1988.

When a marketer is dealing with a wobbler the first step is to review the situation to see, based on the three criteria above, whether there are any possibilities to make a builder of the product. If the answer is 'no', a quick decision to discontinue the line is the most sensible route as otherwise it will just become a parasite and a drain on the company resources. If the answer is 'yes', the second step is to find or create the feedback loops that will enable the marketer to monitor the results of the new marketing activities. The third step is to use the marketing system to push the product in the right direction. This third step is the most critical and also the most difficult, not only from an operational point of view, but it is also important to remain positive and enthusiastic while at the same time keeping a critical eye on the sales development. The positive view is needed to ensure that the product is given a fair chance (a salesperson or customer is unlikely to support a product that is on its way out), while the critical eye is needed to make the right analyses of the progress that is being made.

Most marketers like to see their wobblers succeed; in reality the majority of them will not succeed but will have to be discontinued to avoid becoming a parasite. Ideally the person in charge should have the sensitivity to pick up the 'right' signals from the market in combination with the skills to use the best marketing tools to nudge a product in the right direction, plus a cool analytical mind ready to 'pull the plug' when it is obvious that the product in question does not have a future.

Summary

The concepts of builders, parasites and wobblers introduced in this chapter illustrate the importance of taking care of a company's products and allocating resources to those parts of the range that have the best potential to generate sales and profits. Builders are the backbone of any company, and it is difficult to overestimate the time and effort one should spend on taking care of these products. Parasites, on the other hand, are the products that do not sell and do not generate profits and should be cut out of the range as soon as possible. In dealing with wobblers, the marketer can aim to nudge them in the right direction, not forgetting to monitor their progress very carefully.

13

Product development: creating tomorrow's stars

Product development is an area where the impact of the changing environment has in many instances been greatly misunderstood. It is often assumed that just because we have more rapid information transfers and technological change the real pace of change in product design will change equally quickly and that the customers will change their needs faster than in the past.

Part of understanding change is to realize that different parts of the universe change at different speeds and that although there are common patterns each situation remains unique.

New and old products

From a marketing point of view there is a significant difference between using technology to enhance existing products (old product development, OPD), to launch new versions of existing concepts but within the same brand, and to launch brand new ideas and concepts (new product development, NPD). The changing world makes it more essential than ever to enhance a product's performance constantly to ensure that it continues to offer perceived value for money. To launch brand new concepts and ideas is still a most uncertain activity. It is becoming even more difficult to define correctly the 'right' idea for a new product as, for instance, research results and personal experience tend to 'grow old' more rapidly than in the past.

Within the majority of markets and, in particular those in FMCG, investment in OPD is significantly more profitable than in NPD. The failure rate is lower and the returns are higher. If an innovation is introduced with an existing product, trial is immediate and provided that the innovation really is a step forward the repeat purchases will increase. The 'attachment' to an established product makes failure much less likely, and as the expected growth will come from a much higher base than with a new product the returns will be higher.

The key to success for the many, 'old', products among the best-selling UK FMCG products (an average age of 35 years among the top 20) is constant development. Everything from Heinz Baked Beans and Kellogg's Corn Flakes to Nescafé have undergone significant changes in order to keep their positions as top-selling items. Failing to take care of the products one has in a company is very inefficient and represents a waste of resources.

OPD has one other important effect: it focuses on the main segments of the marketplace rather than niches. It is obvious, but often forgotten, that it is much more efficient to operate in a large market with economies of scale than in a small niche.

It is sometimes argued that it is a 'safe' position to have a strong market share in a small niche, and that in doing so a product or service is perhaps not pleasing so many people but the users stay very loyal and satisfied. Research has indicated that this is not true. Small niche brands within large sectors (at least in the consumer goods industry) do not have a loyal following, rather the reverse. Users of small 'niche' brands are less loyal, their main usage is with the main brands within the market sector, not the niche brand. The niche brand tends to be tied to specific occasions and might well develop occasion-loyalty which can be a sound base for a business but the marketer would be wrong in assuming that the loyalty is built on a more general preference.

EXAMPLE 13.1

Procter & Gamble's Fairy washing-up liquid is an excellent example of how one can, with a very basic product, build a strong market position on steadily improving product performance. Fairy has been advertised in the UK for many years with two alternating messages: kind to the skin and washes more dishes than ordinary washing-up liquids. In the recessionary period of the early 1990s the latter has, of course, been a more powerful message than the former.

The commercial success of the consistent message and product delivery has meant that since its launch in 1959 Fairy has built market share from around 30 per cent in the early 1980s to over 50 per cent by 1992.

While it took seven years to improve the formula in the 1980s (relaunches in 1981 and 1988), during the 1990s the pace has increased. The revised and improved Fairy Excel was launched in 1992, four years after the latest relaunch, and 14 months after the Excel launch the next, upgraded version, called Fairy Excel Plus was introduced.

In the case of Fairy the basic promise has remained the same; the brand is still Fairy and the function of the product is certainly the same, but with the help of rapid product improvements a strong market position has been created.

Another aspect of NPD and OPD is to what extent the investment in R&D should go into product-related development versus the amount spent on process development. A study by MIT in the United States revealed that while the US companies during the 1980s invested two-thirds of the budget in new products and one-third in process development, i.e. how to make the products more efficiently, the Japanese companies spent their money in a totally different way: one-third on new products and two-thirds on process development. In Germany the relationship between the two types of expenditure was 50/50. The conclusion of the study was, not surprisingly, that the higher investment in process improvements in Japan and, to a degree, in Germany had significantly contributed to the success of these countries' industries. Improved perceived value for money, the result of process improvements, has been shown to be more important than novelties.

Money is, of course, not everything; it is the way the money is spent that really makes the difference. During the 1980s the two top spenders on research and development were General Motors and IBM. These two companies share another common feature, and that is record losses. When IBM announced in 1993 that it had made the world's largest financial loss, the record had previously been held by General Motors.

Even though it is essential and a first priority to take care of 'old' products, new product development remains a very important activity. For a company to grow, new ideas need to be developed and the more creative work involved in new products will also benefit existing ones.

Time and speed

The time it takes to bring a product to the marketplace has been the subject of several studies over the past decade. The shorter development time for the Japanese car manufacturers during the

1980s was in many instances quoted as one major reason for their success. While previously it took 6–8 years in the United States to develop a new car, the objective now is to do it in 2–3 years. Similarly, in the consumer electronics industry the Japanese claim to have a much faster product development cycle than Western companies.

If the speed of change is increasing and the competitive situation is increasingly turbulent, it is obvious that faster throughput times for development projects become essential.

EXAMPLE 13.2

In rapidly changing businesses such as telecommunications the difference in timing can be the difference between order or no order. Ericsson, a world leader in telephone exchanges, has cut its development time dramatically by using 'concurrent engineering' rather than sequential development. By using this new system the time from order to delivery of an AXE switching system has been cut from 6 months to 10 days. The impact of fast development in this market is further illustrated by the fact that 30–40 per cent of sales come from products launched over the previous two years.

EXAMPLE 13.3

One of the more well-publicized efforts to cut development time has been Heinz' Weight Watchers frozen prepared meals in the US. By reorganizing the development process, bringing in more teamwork, the development time has been cut from the fairly standard 22 months to half or even in some cases 14 weeks. This has been combined with a large number of new products, for the fiscal year 1993 up to 100, reaching the market.

Speed, however, is not everything. Faster work has not meant that Weight Watchers has gained market share; the share started to slip by the end of 1993 and did not recover in 1994 (at the time of writing). In an intensely competitive market other brands have been more successful. Speed in itself is not a competitive advantage, it is only when it is combined with offering a product or service that is perceived as providing superior value for money to competition that one gets the positive effects.

EXAMPLE 13.4

South-East Asia represents, in certain segments of the FMCG market, an extremely fast-changing market. According to magazine reports, at the Lever Brothers South-East Asia Innovation Haircare Centre in Thailand, haircare products are launched on a monthly basis in the desire to stay brand leader. Rather than spending a lot of time researching the feasibility of a new idea or concept, strategic instinct has taken over as an important resource. Research is mainly used to gather market information and as a check against significant negatives, not to give sales predictions.

Faster working methods must never be an excuse for less quality in the thinking and execution. The quest for perfection must not be compromised. Correctly managed the two dimensions, speed and quality, are not contradictory. With faster feedback loops the information available for action is more relevant as it is fresher, with more rapid development work the information is transformed to action and (test-)sales quicker and in total the outcome should represent an improvement. What the faster throughput times require is a greater awareness among the product development staff of what the market requires and the competitive situation. When concurrent engineering is in place and there are no phased activities, you can start step 5 before step 1 is concluded. Targeting and customer understanding become much more important as you cannot rely on the previous step to guide your work.

The shotgun or the rifle?

Many management authors, such as Tom Peters, argue that in a 'faster' world it is better to use a shotgun approach than the old-fashioned rifle method. With a shotgun approach you launch a number of ideas, and throw them on the market in the hope that something might succeed, the theory being that you cannot predict what the customers will like so you might as well launch as much as you can and hope for the best.

Real-life experience does not support this concept, which is also favoured by some Japanese companies. Too many new ideas at any one time are very expensive as modern distribution and marketing methods require substantial investments to launch a product. It is also confusing for the customers to be exposed to an ungraspable amount of novelties. The targeted rifle approach is still the better as it concentrates resources, it shows respect for the customers' time and operations and it forces discipline into the organization. With the shotgun approach the system is 'asked' to cope with an unnecessary amount of change.

After a decade of intensive launch activity the shotgun companies have been forced to rethink their policies and during the early 1990s most of the consumer goods giants in Japan announced range reductions.

The part of the shotgun approach that the skilled marketer should follow is the careful monitoring of how a product is received. Fast feedback from the marketplace is invaluable when it comes to deciding the amount of resources that should be put behind a launch.

Think globally, develop locally

This version of the well-known management axiom is relevant also in the context of developing products and it is the latter end of the statement that is of primary interest. Global thinking is important when considering options and how to find ideas to move forward, while in most instances closing a business deal is a very local activity.

Many manufacturers are going to great lengths to be able to supply customized products for the customers. Walk into any car showroom and you are overwhelmed with various options you can obtain with your car. Walk into the supermarket and you can design your own pizza to take home with you. The rapidly changing world of manufacturing control is making greater customization possible while retaining important benefits of scale.

In the car industry, BMW has shown that it is possible to sell not only individual variations on cars based on a similar set of techniques, but also to create several different ranges of cars. BMW makes in total 35 different models from the fairly basic 316 to the ultimate luxury cars in the 6- and 7-series from a relatively limited number of parts.

EXAMPLE 13.5

According to magazine reports, the National Bicycle Industrial Company in Kokubu, Japan, builds made-to-order bicycles on an assembly line. The bicycles, each individually designed, are delivered within two weeks of order. The company reportedly offers 11 231 862 variations with a premium price for the customization of only 10 per cent.

These changes have important implications for the marketers; they change the focus of scale economics and allow a combination of mass marketing *and* customization.

The scale economics of business used to depend on manufacturing facilities. In an efficient company, the factory produced similar items so that there were few line changes; raw materials could be purchased in vast quantities; staff would know exactly what they were doing and would be well down the learning curve; and management could focus on getting the best out of the process.

In today's changed world it has become feasible to run a flexible factory efficiently and the scale economics have moved away from the factory. To elaborate on the flexible factory is outside the scope of this book and I have highlighted the issue only to show the potential for locally adapted products, to be able to gain strengths from having a strong position in a local market or, perhaps more correctly, in several local markets.

EXAMPLE 13.6

Nescafé is the leading brand of the Swiss food giant Nestlé and Nescafé is sold across the world. With more communication across borders, the message has become increasingly more consistent from one country to another.

The cross-border flow of commercials and multinational use of commercials, such as the UK 'Gold Blend' couple in several other European countries, has not had any direct impact on that specific product being sold in each country. The Nescafé blends sold in Sweden, France, Italy and the UK are all different, because they have been developed over time separately and they fit into local coffee habits.

The changing pattern of where the economies of scale are generated has an impact on the product development strategy in that even if there is some decrease in the production efficiencies it might well be compensated for by scale effects in other parts of the cost chain. This has always been true, but the changes to the way manufacturing can be run have decreased the penalties of customization while the economies of scale in, for instance, advertising have in many cases increased with globalization. The combination opens up interesting opportunities to gain competitive advantage through production flexibility.

But unlimited product proliferation under one brand is not necessarily good marketing management practice, the strategy outlined above has to fit the market 'mentality'. The above refer mainly to regional differentiation rather than several versions being on sale within one market sector. 'Unnecessary' range extensions tend to destabilize a brand's position as the product development factor takes a prominent place in the marketing mix, disloyalty to one particular product is encouraged due to the temptation to try new versions and local benefits of scale in distribution disappears. The marketing maxim that 'choice breeds disloyalty' still applies.

In the marketing strategy, and in particular the product development strategy, one has to differentiate clearly between technical development, product development and brand development.

- *Technical development*—that is, improving a product's performance in the widest sense of the word—is of universal importance but does not necessarily need to be channelled through a new product. Enhancing an existing product is in most cases a much more effective way of utilizing an invention.
- *Product development*—that is, launching new products within existing brand concepts, can be dealt with separately from brand development. Most products live for quite some time and in most markets opportunities exist for profitable activities.
- *Brand development* is something different; it is sometimes tied to a product and sometimes not and does not really belong to this chapter, but it is mentioned here to reinforce the point that good brands can live forever and the life of a brand does not follow any life cycle.

Technical innovation has a limited life and product versions have an equally limited life. Product concepts that fulfil a certain function have a very long life and brands can live for as long as they are taken care of properly.

The product life cycle theory

The product life cycle theory has haunted the marketing profession ever since it was first brought into the management debate in the early 1960s. It has been used as a rationale by brand managers over the years—in many cases wrongly—and given the amount of change we are facing, it is essential to understand fully the difference between the product life cycle theory and marketing.

The theory says that all products go through a number of phases: introduction/market development, growth, maturity and decline. The theory is a dangerous tool in that it uses terminology that is incorrect and can easily be misunderstood.

The theory has led many marketing executives astray as it mixes up technical development with brand and product development. The theory in itself was originally based on mainly industrial products with limited marketing support in the early 1960s and has since been misquoted in a number of instances. These products represented executions of technical solutions which undoubtedly go through something that resembles a life cycle.

The life cycle of a product is something totally different, as a product is created to fulfil certain requirements and it represents a company's ability to solve this. The customer 'habit' is unlikely to change; the product can well remain the same although the product execution might change a number of times.

For the same reasons, but more pronounced, brands do not have a predetermined life cycle. A well-managed brand can live for ever and there are several examples to support this. As an example, 'Stradivarius' on a violin was a good brand in the eighteenth century and is an even better one now. In more modern times, Ford has been a good car brand since the introduction of the mass-produced model T in 1909, and it remains a world leader. In the UK consumer goods industry we have brands such as Whitbread and Cadbury with heritages going back over 150 years.

Many development projects have been started because (marketing) management has analysed the product portfolio and come to the conclusion that many products are in the 'mature' stage. On the basis of that they have started development projects to take the company into new 'growth' sectors or, alternatively, to buy companies in growth markets. In many or most cases this has led to mistakes and loss of profits as resources have been channelled from taking care of existing big-sellers to new products that have failed.

The only thing the theory supports is that a technical solution to a product feature is likely to be short-lived and needs to be replaced in due course. A product as a concept does not go through the life cycle unless mismanaged and, similarly, a brand has nothing at all to do with the theory.

A product as a concept does, sometimes, go through the first stages described in the cycle as it is often first picked up by 'innovators' and it does generate market growth. After a period the growth rate might decline as the primary saturation is filled. If a marketer at that stage concludes that 'this product will soon start to decline' and puts the emphasis on other products the conclusion will become a self-fulfilling prophecy. If, on the other hand, the marketer sets about to further enhance and improve the perceived value of the product through communication, 'soft ware' or further technical improvements, the product will continue to prosper and grow.

EXAMPLE 13.7

The automobile is a typical example of a product that has gone through a number of changes over the years, but the basic function is the same now as it was at the beginning of the century (the very first cars from Benz and Co were perhaps something different).

In the mechanics of making the car, technical innovations have come and gone, in most instances making the final product better value for money. These technical solutions have sometimes been apparent, such as in the case of the automatic gearbox, and sometimes not, such as the change to electronic ignition. In all cases they illustrate the need for constant rejuvenation in order to maintain the business, which is what successful companies do.

The life cycle for the automobile is virtually indefinite and certainly over the last 100 years the curve has been upwards almost all the time.

From a product development point of view the conclusion is that it is essential not to mix the technical development needs with the launch of new products and brands. The development activities are needed to enhance what is on the market and, if appropriate, to launch new concepts—the latter in particular if the competition changes, when the customers become more well informed or the external forces are changing the circumstances in which one is competing. If the sales of a product are no longer increasing the reason is more likely to be that the competitive edge has disappeared because the competition has improved than that the product has entered some sort of predetermined decline.

Provided a product fulfils a universal need, such as moving people, quenching thirst or calculating, the product will live more or less for ever. The best quote regarding the life cycle concept is: 'The product life cycle theory is just a good excuse for bad marketing.'

Create uniqueness

Few marketers need to be reminded of the advantages that follow from having a unique product. A unique feature, provided it has a positive value to the customers, can allow premium pricing, access to distribution channels, etc., enforcing the links between supplier and customer.

Sometimes the uniqueness can be a complicated formula based on technological breakthroughs, such as in the pharmaceutical industry; sometimes it is based on 'hard work' to make a product just marginally but decisively better; and sometimes the solution is apparent to everyone but no one has the 'guts' to pursue it. The launch of the round tea bag in the UK falls into the last category.

EXAMPLE 13.8

In the mid-1980s Tetley tea bags were No. 2 in a market that was getting increasingly competitive; the brand was slowly losing share to cheaper own label tea bags.

One option that was investigated was a round, rather than square, teabag. After several years of process development, a 'kit' was developed in the greatest secrecy to convert the existing tea bag machines to producing round bags.

The round tea bag was launched in mid-1989 and within 18 months Tetley had increased its business by 30 per cent and moved from being No. 2 to brand leader with a 3–4 per cent margin over the former No. 1.

The increased ability to manage shorter production runs, mentioned in the previous section, has opened up opportunities for different 'cosmetic' line extensions in the form of limited editions. Originally this was something that belonged to the art world where, for instance, a lithograph would only be available in 100 copies, after which the printing stones would be destroyed. The wine estates have used similar techniques in that only limited amounts have been allowed to be produced under the 'proper' label according to the *appelation controlée* rules.

The practice has spread to a number of consumer goods industries, perhaps most effectively marketed by the car companies. Limited editions of Minis, Renault 5s, Volvos, Ford Escorts, etc., have been brought to the market with good results.

EXAMPLE 13.9

The most profitable limited edition sales are built on exploiting a collector's market, such as in the case of art or even wine. The trend towards collecting Levi's jeans led the Levi Strauss company to launch a special edition of the famous 501 model in early 1994. Levi's with a big E on the label were, according to market specialists, a collector's item, often selling for up to £200. This indicated an interest—and by staying in touch with the market this was picked up—and a new limited edition, in the same design, was brought out at a retail price in the US of $100.

A more specific way of creating uniqueness is to produce and market executions of a product tailored for a specific market sector or region.

A more multicultural society in many parts of Europe due to migration from poorer countries to the richer has meant that the target groups are less homogeneous not only when it comes to the more subtle cultural issues but also in simple matters such as language. By providing translations on a consumer pack or machine instructions a company can gain a competitive advantage.

Another way of using the same techniques, but for a totally different purpose, is to produce different varieties of the same product under different brands for different distribution channels. In the grocery trade this has often been a route for companies who want to supply one retailer without upsetting another. For example, in order to supply a low margin discounter, a company might choose to produce a product in a different pack weight. By doing so the traditional price comparison, pack for pack across different channels, will be more difficult and the producer will avoid discussions regarding more or less competitive price levels. One example is that ALDI in Germany for many years sold their 'own' pack size of After Eight chocolate mints to avoid price comparisons with the more traditional retailers.

A third way of building business in a turbulent world is to use the improved feedback loops to develop new products. With a more rapidly changing environment the necessity for better feedback can not only help the company's operations, it can also grow into new products.

EXAMPLE 13.10

The production of electricity is an activity that depends to a large extent on feedback. When producing such a commodity that cannot be saved and you do not know until afterwards what the exact production pattern has been, the production control needs to build up a thorough understanding of the customer base.

In Nacka, a large community just outside Stockholm, Sweden, the electricity company has moved this thinking one step further. The most expensive electricity to produce is the peak demand. The top units of electricity can cost as much as 120 times the average, so if one can cut the peaks significant savings can be made.

The Nacka electricity company has developed a feedback system with its main customers so that they can track in detail each unit's consumption. Different customers have, of course, different abilities to change their consumption pattern but if, for instance, electricity is used for heating, you can slow down for an hour in a big system without any problems providing you can turn it on again at full power later.

When the company's feedback loops start to indicate that a peak in consumption is on its way, the company contacts the main customers and asks them to pull back. By building up a 'feel' for when the peaks will come, they can balance the consumption and avoid the very expensive maximum peak production levels.

By using this know-how Nacka has created a new product which saves the utility money which is shared with the main customers who help them achieve their goal.

Summary

Product development will continue to play an important part in the marketing mix. In a turbulent world it is more advisable, particularly for a leading company, to continue to use the new technology for the existing product portfolio, ensuring that the market positions and supplier–customer links that have been built up remain strong.

Technological advances make more financially viable opportunities available to create locally adapted products, special editions and other small runs, not only for the smaller companies but in particular for the larger ones with strong brands. They can use their economies of scale in communication to support activity at the local level with customized products and services.

Technical advances are in the main destabilizing, but they also move markets forward. The pace of change in itself is not stable; periods of rapid change can be followed by limited change and vice versa. No company can afford to ignore product development; to be a leader also implies leadership in development. The technical advances can, however, be used in different ways depending on a company's position and objectives in a market.

14

Sales promotions

Achieving the illusive sales increase

Sales promotions of various sorts take a significant part of any marketer's budget and responsibility. Not all brands and products can fund large advertising campaigns or even have product development programmes, but I have yet to meet a brand manager who does not have a promotions budget.

Sales promotions have over the last 10–15 years taken an increasingly larger share of the marketing budgets, mainly at the expense, in relative terms, of media advertising. This trend has been particularly pronounced in the United States where in 1977 the relationship between advertising and promotions was 60/40, and just 10 years later it was 40/60.

A sales promotion activity usually has one main objective—to achieve a sales increase in the short term—and several secondary ones such as building brand loyalty, to counter a competitive initiative and/or to bring in new customers. While these objectives usually make sense and are credible, it is the experience of many marketers that they are very difficult to achieve, especially in mature markets.

The main and real purpose behind most promotions is not so much to offer the customer something interesting or even to change the value-for-money perception, it is to break through the 'noise level' in the marketplace. At the most basic level, the aim may be to give the salesforce or sales agents something to talk to the customers about, i.e. breaking through the internal barriers, or to ensure that one's products are displayed properly in a supermarket or department store.

Promotions have, generally speaking, a different effect depending on where in the supply chain a company is operating. The comments above, and those that follow, are mainly made from the perspective of the manufacturing industry. For the retail trade the conclusions as to the effects are, at least partially, different. The direct effect appears to be more advantageous for the promoter, and the indirect image effects are in many cases much more positive than they are for a manufacturer. Most successful retailers have very aggressive programmes, and contrary to the manufacturing business, several successful and profitable operations, such as IKEA, Hennes, Tesco and Kwiksave, have been built on a strong pricing platform, admittedly in combination with a strong product and image message.

Promotional activities form one of the main tools a marketer can use to create instability in a market, as outlined previously. Especially aggressive price promotions are likely to destabilize the marketing system and, given the relative increase in promotional spend, many companies have, apparently unknowingly, only themselves to blame for a less loyal customer base.

The price variable

The most common promotional tool is the price promotion and it is not unusual that price promotions form one of the largest, if not the largest, part of the marketing budget.

Setting the right price is almost an art in itself, and deciding how to deal with pricing in a promotional context is not much easier. Whatever route one takes one can be sure that discount levels once introduced to a customer will be very difficult to decrease. It also takes a lot of experience to set the discount levels so that the company gets the maximum effect from a promotion.

The importance of getting it right is easily illustrated by the fact that a 1 per cent increase in the net sales value will result in a net profit increase of 10 per cent if the net margin is 10 per cent, and of course the calculation is as powerful in reverse; a 1 per cent decrease will lead to a 10 per cent decrease in profitability.

The compartmentalizing of many companies has meant that in reality the price promotion variable is appearing in many different guises. We have the short-term price promotions often controlled via the marketing budget, but we also have in most companies a wide range of various types of bonuses, all of which will influence the final price to the customers. Those bonuses can be a reflection of savings in the supplying company, such as pallet discounts and full-load discounts, or a reflection of the negotiation situation, such as year-end bonuses. If the company is selling its products on the basis of free delivery, there is a further hidden discount to the companies that are situated at some distance in that they do not pay their 'fair' part of the transportation costs.

This complex structure is seen as a problem by many executives, and so it can be from a control point of view, but it also represents an opportunity in that the multitude of discount formats open up possibilities for improving the effectiveness of the spent or 'given away' pound sterling. In most cases the sensitivity to a change of the different types of discounts differs and the alert company can 'play the game' so that when discounts are withdrawn, this is done in the least sensitive areas, and when they are introduced they are put into the type of expenditure where the sales and customer relation effects will be maximized. In a case quoted in the *Harvard Business Review*, one company in the technical household appliance sector in the United States increased its average unit revenue over 12 months by 3.5 per cent, while getting a volume increase of 11 per cent and a total profit improvement of 60 per cent by using this technique.

The effectiveness of price promotions is something that has been debated between sales managers and marketers for as long as marketing departments have existed. In at least some cases the investment in a price promotion is repaid immediately due to the extra sales, and in such a case there is little need for a discussion as to the usefulness of the activity. In other situations, such as in the grocery retail trade, the power relationship between supplier and distributor is forcing the suppliers to keep promoting in order to keep the business, and again there is little point in discussing the finer strategic points as promotions have then become a necessity and part of the overall business reasons for supplying a certain retailer. In some instances—for example, in a fully integrated operation with selling and manufacturing under its own control—it is distinctly possible to optimize the promotional programme on the basis of achieving the best financial results, without taking 'power-relationships' into account.

An argument that is often used to warrant price promotions is that with a price promotion in a shop, new buyers are attracted to the brand. By getting new buyers to try the product they will become future loyal customers. This hypothesis has been analysed thoroughly by Professor Ehrenberg of the London Business School, particularly to discover if it applies to established big brands in the FMCG industry. The conclusion of the survey covering around 100 brands in 25 product categories in four countries (UK, USA, Japan and Germany) was that consumer promotions (mainly price related) for established brands of FMCG products have no noticeable effect either on subsequent sales levels or on brand loyalty. The measured difference in sales between and after a promotion in the UK was 1 per cent and in the US, was as close to zero as one can expect.

The reason for the lack of long-term effect is that the extra sales the promotions generated came largely from previous customers of the brands. In other words, the sales growth was not an effect of new customers 'discovering' brand X, it was an effect of previously lapsed buyers returning when the product is on sale, offering better value for money. Around 70–80 per cent of the new buyers during the promotion period had actually bought the brand in the previous 6–12 month period.

Because the 'new' customers were disloyal in coming to brand X, they are also likely to be disloyal in the future, moving away when a better offer is available somewhere else. From this we can assume that the greater the amount of product sold on price promotions in a market, the more disloyal will the customers be and the more unstable will the market system be.

From time to time companies declare that they will do away with short-term price promotions and work on an everyday low price formula instead. The reasons for this are usually very logical and rational: price promotions cost money to administer, they impose a purchasing pattern on the customers and they cause logistical problems with the suppliers. Depending on the market position and a brand's inherent strengths, the effect can be dramatically different.

If a brand is, to a relatively large extent, dependent on price promotions for its sales volume, an everyday low price philosophy will probably lead to decreasing sales. On the other hand, if the brand has a strong normal sales pattern, sales will increase. Research from the US suggests that if a brand switches from price cuts to everyday low price it will lose brand share and sales over the following 12 to 24 months. The reason is probably that it takes some time for the customers to change their perceptions, moving from the more volatile price-focused environment to the more stable non-promotional one. During the phase when the instability is still in the system, the company is likely to lose share unless significant investments are made in stabilizing the market quickly.

The pricing variable is an integral part of the marketing mix as well as the promotional mix. It has a direct impact on profitability from the point of view of income generation and in boosting or losing sales. Understanding the chaos implications will hopefully enhance the opportunities to use this variable for the intended purposes.

Non-price promotions

A lot of effort and money are spent every year on building non-price-related promotional programmes. These might include competitions, free offers, cross promotions, etc. Sometimes there is a genuine idea behind the activity, such as the Heinz charity collection schemes; and sometimes the activity seems to be constructed more in order to give the salespersons something to talk about with their contacts and the buyers an excuse for getting a free gift. The following refers to the former, not the latter.

Consumer promotions that genuinely serve to build a relationship with the customers will fulfil the same function as other types of communication such as advertising. A message that generates interest and action and purveys positive value dimensions is, of course, an effective contributor to the brand equity.

In order to be successful not only do the objectives and the strategies have to mirror the brand image, the execution must be consistent. The risks of a consumer promotion going wrong is significant; it is easy to misjudge what the exact effects of a specific offer will be. When the promotional activities are limited to well-known types of activities such as coupons or free offers in a previously tried format, it is fairly easy to predict the outcome with a reasonable amount of accuracy (exact forecasting is, as explained earlier, an impossibility). When a company tries something new and bold, the risks increase.

One of the most spectacular mistakes of this type was the UK Hoover promotion in the autumn and winter of 1992–93. The net result of the promotion was a cost to the company of over £20 million plus an effect on reputation which is difficult to evaluate.

EXAMPLE 14.1

The Hoover promotion ran in two stages. Stage one, during the early autumn of 1992, offered customers two free return air tickets to continental Europe if they purchased any Hoover product worth more than £100. Stage two, which began on 1 November, was an offer of two free flights to the United States if the customers purchased a Hoover product worth more than £250.

Stage one of the promotion started off fairly well with satisfied customers and little general attention. It was only months after the promotion had ended that adverse comments started to appear.

Stage two was almost instantly a news story. The Hoover promotion was not the first of its kind, several companies had run free flight promotions previously but without the attention and side-effects Hoover was soon to experience. The Hoover promotion caught the imagination of people, especially when alert journalists realized that the company had not made any commitments as to how they would send the participants in the promotion over the Atlantic. Then, they started to fuel doubts as to how the details of the promotion were designed. The promotion was created so that prospective participants would be discouraged to go through the whole process. One such aspect was that there were six steps to be taken, five by post, within eight weeks to obtain the free tickets. The customers were expected to tire of the process and not bother to complete the offer. In the case of Hoover that did not happen.

In addition, the company also misjudged the way the customers would respond to the offer. Normally one would expect a 5–10 per cent redemption rate; the Hoover promotion went significantly over that.

The end result was that a large number of appliances were sold but the costs to the company proved to be enormous. The attention to detail that is necessary in a turbulent world was missed and safeguards to allow for the unpredictability of the consumers were not installed— actually the reverse, as apparently no tickets at all were purchased prior to the promotion.

The Hoover promotion is not the only one to go wrong, it is just the most spectacular in the UK in 'living memory'. The lessons are universally applicable however, and in the future the faster communication systems and the more sophisticated and fickle consumers will make proper awareness of the potential for uncontrolled behaviour in any system even more of a necessity.

Understanding promotional behaviour

Sales promotion activities are by nature a dimension in the marketing mix which, when related to pricing, is more likely to create instability, and when the promotions are of a thematic character they can actually stabilize a system. As discussed previously, this can be to a company's advantage or disadvantage, depending on the circumstances, but awareness of the effects is a necessity for profitable business development in a changing world.

Accepting that the main purpose with a promotion is to create extra sales, the important question is how to achieve this most effectively.

As the majority of promotions are price related one can observe that the best sales result is likely to occur when the marketing system is relatively volatile. If there is 'unrest in the system', an aggressive attack can create much higher sales than in a more stable situation as it is more likely that the company can break the links between the competitors and their customers.

This rule is, however, not universal. If, for instance, a brand leader decides to promote aggressively while in the past having been quite passive in this respect, the effect is probably quite dramatic. The short-term sales uplift is likely to be significant as the main brand will have more latent purchasers than the smaller brands. The probable long-term effect, however, is an increase in the total instability and in order to maintain market position the higher promotional spend will need to become a regular feature.

Understanding the chaos marketing concepts makes it easier to isolate these moments in the marketplace, and with rapid decision-making systems it might be possible to use it to one's advantage. These moments of change can be caused by activities such as a new product launch or another major initiative. In a seasonal industry the volatility is particularly pronounced in the early part of the season, and that is the time when it is easier to change brand loyalties.

Correctly used, the momentum a competitor brings to a market sector can be moulded by the brand leader to its advantage. It is not unusual that competitive threats can make the responsive brand leader even stronger because it has been proactive and has taken advantage of the turmoil to convert customers or increase consumption.

EXAMPLE 14.2

The dehydrated soups/sauces market in Europe is dominated by three large companies: Unilever (Batchelors, Blue Bond), CPC (Knorr) and Nestlé (Maggi). Historically only Unilever and CPC were active in the Swedish market, plus a few smaller local producers.

In the early 1980s Nestlé decided to launch a range of dehydrated sauces in Sweden, utilizing the Nestlé know-how from the European continent and challenging Unilever and CPC. The Nestlé launch was heavily supported with advertising as well as price promotions. To protect their market position Unilever mounted a counter-attack.

These more intensive marketing activities from Unilever in combination with the Nestlé spend led, somewhat surprisingly, to a stronger position for Unilever. The gain was not really due to any loss of share by Nestlé, as they had none prior to the launch, but from the other competitors.

The result was that the main beneficiary of the Nestlé launch was Unilever, Nestlé itself did not really gain a foothold. It was perhaps less surprising that the increase in marketing activity led to market growth.

Using seasonality to increase sales is a classic technique. A primary example of extending a seasonal product is the Cadbury cream eggs (chocolate-coated confectionery 'eggs'). The eggs were originally sold only at Easter—for obvious reasons—but over time the season has been extended more and more so that the eggs are now available almost all year round.

When planning sales promotion activities the main tactic is usually to ensure that one has the best 'slots' at the peak buying time. An alternative approach is to increase the activity at the low season, to operate a counter-cyclical activity. Although this might generate less sales in total, it can, depending on the competitive scenario, be more profitable as less discounts might be required.

A more flexible view of the seasonality can generate excellent ideas of how to sell more in a profitable way. The marketing system might be more receptive to the activities of a smaller company in the off-season and sharp activities can create useful instability which the main brand might not be able to counter.

It is, of course, unwise to consider the off-season possibilities before one is satisfied that the peak periods do not offer a more profitable opportunity. Especially for a leading brand it is preferable in most cases to operate within the parameters of a system rather than breaking it, but both possibilities should be considered.

The timing of a promotion can also be related to the correct environment. The way an offer is presented will influence the potential customer's receptiveness.

EXAMPLE 14.3

A key objective in the activity of many car dealers is to get trial, i.e. to get the main target group into the showroom and behind the wheel. In the case of the more expensive cars, it is not unusual to lend a prospective customer the car for a day. Although the possibility to do so is open to almost everyone, a skilful presentation of the offer is much more likely to generate a significant response.

In 1992 the recession had hit the car industry very badly, and sales had dropped by 30 per cent since 1989. BMW decided to try a different approach; rather than just inviting people to come to a BMW showroom to test the car, the offer was made part of a sales promotion activity with targeted publications.

One such programme was to offer the 40 000 readers of the trade journal *Financial Advisor* the possibility to borrow a 5-series BMW for a day, an offer that was picked up by 1000 financial executives. Another approach was to transform the offer to an incentive. If someone wanted to join the distribution list of *Financial Director* magazine, another trade journal, that person would get the use of a BMW for one day. The cost to the company was very low, reportedly £25 000, but the quality of the leads was very good and the cost-effectiveness much higher than in the more traditional way of achieving trial.

The multiplier effect that was introduced earlier in the book can be used also in the context of sales promotion. By coordinating activities across the spectrum of the marketing mix, the total effect will be more than the sum of the parts. For instance, according to magazine reports, Coca-Cola has, not surprisingly, concluded that a 20 per cent price cut on its own is less effective than a 10 per cent cut in combination with a total in-store package with theme display and advertising support.

EXAMPLE 14.4

Gaymer's Olde English Cider used an unusual approach to gain extra sales and new customers during the summer of 1992: a combination of targeted direct mail and radio advertising.

The target group for the activity was younger men, aged 25–44, and the region for the activity was London where the radio station Capital Gold provided a suitable audience profile. The radio commercials were backed with a 300 000 mail drop. To select the target group all households with men in the age group were identified. The next step was to isolate those in the age group who were regular or heavy users of cider and, finally, households outside the catchment area of shops carrying Olde English were excluded.

The combination of targeted radio advertising with a well-defined direct mail drop with a leaflet, a money-off coupon and an invitation to enter a Capital Gold competition resulted in a high coupon redemption level (four times the industry average) and an increase in market share, from 1.5 per cent to 4 per cent.

Using price promotions to destabilize a system is one way of looking at how the marketing relations are influenced by changes. One can take another view of the same issue and take the system into consideration when selecting the area in which to spend promotional funds. With such an approach one can conclude that a stable market with considerable advertising expenditure is less likely to be an effective market sector for promotional funds while, in the opposite case, a market with a lot innovation and change is more likely to respond to pricing activities.

This theoretical hypothesis matches well the experiences of many marketers. The effect of price-related sales promotions is usually significantly higher in growing markets, particularly those fuelled by new product development activity, than in mature or even declining ones. The strategy to spend oneself out of a declining market has often been tried but seldom with successful results. The previously quoted research by Professor Ehrenberg supports this view.

The rapidly changing market shares in the personal computer market illustrate this point. It is a market segment that has seen significant new product development activities, and during the early 1990s that was matched with heavy price promotions. The results have been a fluctuating picture in brand shares.

One note of warning is that it is useful to distinguish between long-term strategies and tactical short-term moves. For a brand leader in a fairly stable market, it can tactically pay to counter aggressive pricing activity in the short term and handle the potential instability at that stage while it is still graspable, rather than rely solely on stabilizing competitive measures which can be too slow in combating a challenger.

For the marketer the conclusions are that promotional monies are more likely to be well spent in growing and expanding markets than in stable and mature ones. Heavy expenditure in an established market is likely to lead to declining loyalties due to increased instability.

Technological advances

In a book with frequent references to a rapidly changing business environment and covering the subject of sales promotions, it is impossible not to mention the practical effects that technology is bringing to the marketplace.

For instance, in the retail trade the scanning system—particularly when connected to a card programme—offers a wide variety of promotional opportunities. It can, for instance, be used to induce purchasers of one company's products to try the competition. The mechanics are simple: when the computer registers a purchase of brand X, a coupon is issued for the purchase of brand Y. Another way of using the computer and scanning technology is to offer multiple purchase discounts, i.e. if someone buys three packs, x pence is automatically deducted from the bill when pack number 3 passes the scanner. This can also be used for cross purchase: for example, if you buy a pack of fish fingers, you get a discount on the french fried potatoes.

Computer technology is also making various card loyalty schemes a feasible operation. For instance, almost all airlines operate some sort of programme to encourage repeat purchases and reward frequent travellers.

In this context one also has to make a reference to the emergence of electronic media with increasing possibilities to interactive communication. This opens up new commercial possibilities straddling sales promotion, advertising and even the 'normal' sales function.

At the Time Warner multimedia showcase in Orlando, Florida, the viewers act as their own editors. To persuade the viewers to watch the commercials, they receive an instant reward in the form of a coupon when the advert is on the screen. In other words, the advertisers are paying the viewers to watch. This would seem to be a sign of ultimate marketing failure as it is almost like friends paying you to visit them. The total message is that the senders consider the commercial as being of so limited interest that incentives are needed for the customers to watch it.

From a more positive angle one can note that the technique does open up new avenues, providing information flow tailored to individual viewer's circumstances, such as not just a coupon but also the address where one can find the products, usage ideas, addresses for further information, etc.

It is easy to be hypnotized by technology and the opportunities it offers. It is another string on the creative 'bow' of the sales promotional agencies and the marketing departments. However, the technology must never take over when it comes to message and professionalism; the machine is never better than the person controlling it. Using the technology in a positive way and, in particular, to get feedback as fast as possible within the framework of sound brand management is likely to be the most successful approach.

Summary

Sales promotions form an emotive subject. It is a subject in which almost all marketers get involved and it is difficult to get it right. Even if the objectives and strategies are often well thought through it is far from unusual for the outcome of the promotion to be quite different from that intended. The unpredictability of the marketing system is showing through.

The most important points for successful sales promotion activity are to have fast feedback loops, to learn from experience and to take the opportunities to test the procedures. Even though a test situation will never be representative, it can indicate what will happen and faults in programme designs can be discovered before it is too late.

Profitable sales promotion programmes come from creativity and experience. Fine tuning and repeating promotion concepts will lead to increased profits. Sensitivity in handling the price variable can give surprisingly positive effects.

An understanding of the dynamics of the price dimension in a turbulent world is essential to get the maximum impact of price promotions and to evaluate challengers' strategies. Mistakes can generate a chaos system that is out of control.

15

Communication: the intangible link

The main purpose of this chapter is to look at some of the general issues regarding communication, the following chapters will look at main types of communication in more detail.

Communicating with customers is obviously an indispensable part of the marketing mix. If the customers are not told about the product, how can they buy it? At its most basic, the communication flow is nothing but informing potential customers of a product's key factors: what it is. Of course, the use of communication in a proactive sense requires much more than that. Factual information and emotional arguments can create bridges from the supplier to the customer, relationships that will build into strong links, creating friendship-like bonds between seller and buyer.

Businesses communicate with their customers in many different ways. Traditionally, when one mentions communications most marketers think in terms of advertising, but there are many other ways of maintaining a dialogue, or monologue, with the target audience.

From the perspective of chaos and the rapidly changing environment there are several aspects to be aware of in addition to the more traditional ones. First, communication can be used as a tool in the marketing system, usually to stabilize the system. In other words, communication has effects other than just transferring a message from the sender to the recipient. Secondly, the means of communication, the media, is one of the sectors of the marketing world that is experiencing a most rapid change. The advent of electronic 'highways' at one end of the spectrum to the growth in cable and satellite television at the other does make the implementation process more dynamic and even more complicated, as will be illustrated in Chapter 17. Thirdly, the most effective way to communicate is changing in parallel with or at least in the same direction as the general business environment. A message that is in harmony with the recipients' value systems is much more likely to be well received than one that is either outdated or too avant garde for the target audience.

I have deliberately used the expression 'communication' rather than advertising as the latter is only one aspect of how a company can communicate. PR, direct mail and personal contacts/selling are other examples, even the pack design of an FMCG product is part of the communication package.

Communication as a stabilizing influence

In the earlier part of the book the theory of why communication is a stabilizing dimension was described and explained. It is not the intention to repeat those arguments here but to look at communication from a more operational angle.

All types of communication have a stabilizing influence but it appears that the traditional communication methods, advertising and personal selling, have the strongest effects. This is not only because of the nature of the establishment of these relationships, there is also the additional effect of the economies of scale in these two disciplines, although the latter is more a hypothesis than a statement of fact.

The stabilizing influence has to be reviewed from two aspects. There is the direct effect of the activity on the marketing system *and* there is the conclusion that most effective communication programmes are variations on a theme, i.e. consistency in execution creates 'extra' stability.

The former aspect has been reviewed earlier but the latter requires some elaboration as it can appear to contradict the current trend of the media marketplace with its emphasis on new technologies and change. Going back 100 years, the customers were only exposed to a deluge of commercial messages when they visited a town centre or a market. Today, almost everywhere we go we are subjected to the same exposure to commercial messages as our forebears had on their annual trip to the market. It is claimed that the average US consumer is exposed to 3000 commercial messages per day. In addition, each message is getting shorter, and sharper. In the United States the number of 15-second commercials during prime time television increased from 6 per cent in 1985 to 38 per cent in 1988.

A superficial conclusion might be that in such an environment it is necessary to change the message and the execution constantly in order to stay ahead. Drawing conclusions from successful advertising—mainly in consumer goods—the opposite is true. Familiarity, not only with the brand but with the type of message, appears to be a virtue. Famous examples are the Oxo family, the Andrex puppy, Heineken's refreshment approach and, of course, Fairy Liquid, Daz and Persil.

EXAMPLE 15.1

Some of the most criticized advertising is in the detergents sector. Brands such as Daz hammer home, day in and day out, the message that Daz washes whiter than other detergents. The advertising obviously works as otherwise it would not continue to be on air.

The advertising formula where a housewife is asked to test and compare Daz with her ordinary washing powder, also known as the Daz doorstep challenge, originated in the United States. Procter & Gamble had the first version on air in the UK in 1962. Over the interim period of more than 30 years, the commercials have been variations on the same theme. Spokespersons have changed, the executional detail has followed the trends in society and P&G has even ventured into having male endorsers of Daz, but the core message remains unchanged.

An interesting aspect is that over time the product formulation has changed several times. There has been considerably more activity in changing the product than changing the advertising.

The other aspect of the importance of communication development is that consistency in the execution of the message becomes a fundamental part of the strategy. This is a standard 'textbook' marketing discipline but it deserves to be emphasized because communication as such is more efficient if it is executed in a consistent way. The other aspect is that a stabilizing factor is unlikely to work as such unless it is itself fairly stable. There is a double effect to be aware of in creating and executing communication programmes. The dimension as such is, as a rule, stabilizing and by running creative programmes that are consistent, this stabilizing influence is further enhanced.

The conclusion from above, that communication needs to be consistent, is of course not the same as 'not changing'. The most effective systems are those that move forward dynamically and communication has to be treated in the same way. Communication programmes must be rejuvenated, must move forward but must always build on the previous work. The customers have, as a rule, been exposed to the previous creative executions and the new work has to be seen in the context of these previous perceptions.

This is the rule of thumb; that is what the big and successful FMCG companies are doing with brands such as Persil, Whiskas and Fairy Liquid and what successful financial institutions such as the Prudential are doing.

The exceptions are of relevance when the system needs to change, one of the more well-known cases being Guinness in the 1980s, described in Chapter 10. In the case of Guinness the previous creative concept became less and less relevant to the core target group and a total change was necessary to re-establish the brand's credentials.

For communication to work in the way it is intended attention to detail is very important. We know that marginal differences in execution can make the difference between failure and success. A marginal improvement can make a campaign a little bit better than the competitor's and thus sway the consumers in one specific direction.

Many companies fall down on taking care of the details. In a book by Tom Rayfield (*Dear Sir or Madam*), the response companies gave to members of the public (i.e. the author of the book and his wife) replying to advertisements is recorded: 8.5 per cent never replied and a further 15.5 per cent took more than 12 days to give an answer; of those responding 22 per cent got the name and/or address wrong, and only 65 per cent had the sense to follow up the initial enquiry. If one also considers that for many companies a 10 per cent increase or decrease in sales can represent the difference between success and failure the importance of attention to detail is obvious, even when not considering the more strategic implications. The fact that the research was carried out in 1993, a year of recession, shows that many companies have a lot to learn.

While communication will stabilize a marketing system to the advantage of the sender, one has to keep a realistic mind as to what communication actually can achieve. It is not the intention to go into the pros and cons of what is achievable and review the details of the communication process, but it is relevant to remember that it is very difficult to change social attitudes and behaviour in a general sense. For years governments across the world have been spending money on informing the public about the dangers of smoking and excessive drinking and, lately, on the dangers of 'unsafe' sex. According to a World Health Authority review of 150 campaigns 'measurable changes in attitudes ... (and) behaviour are comparatively rare'.

This is consistent with chaos systems thinking in that communication can only 'push' the behaviour if there is a change going on 'anyway'. Additional communication which fits the current trends can boost the changes in society from a message as well as from an adaptation point of view and make the changes more rapid but it is unlikely that any basic attitudes will shift just because of media communication.

It is more important in communication than in most other areas of the marketing realm that the technical progress is looked at separately from the conceptual. Technical change can bring about a number of new opportunities such as improving the product or improving communication techniques and targeting. The conceptual part of the process remains unchanged; we like to feel familiar with the products and the brands. The reputation we are building has to be built on the same foundations as personal relationships, and most people prefer their friends to stay roughly the same over time or, perhaps more correctly, to develop at the same rate as themselves. They became your friends because you had something in common, but if one part changes more than the other then the basis for friendship has disappeared.

Communication is a stabilizing factor in the marketing mix; it is the tool most likely to be used successfully by brand leaders to retain a strong position. To do so in the most successful way usually requires consistency and careful progressive development without losing any identity or wasting past investments in 'good will'.

Crisis management

Crisis management is a subject that has become more top of mind in recent years. The combination of terrorist attacks and more vulnerable infrastructures because of technological progress has meant that many companies have elaborate plans to deal with the unexpected. The following are just a few aspects of this subject, looking at the issue from a marketing angle.

Crisis management involves two distinct aspects: on the one hand, preparing a company for disruptions to the operations; on the other, to put plans in place to deal with unexpected demands from a communication point of view.

EXAMPLE 15.2

The IRA attack on the City of London on Friday 10 April hit the insurance company Commercial Union's head office. The CU management of this crisis is a perfect example of crisis marketing management.

The explosion took place at 21.20, the first crisis meeting was held at 22.00, only 20 minutes after the news of the explosion had been on television, and by midnight the disaster recovery plan was activated. Issues at stake were, for instance, how to reinstate 3600 telephone lines by Monday morning, how to accommodate 650 staff, how to provide them with the necessary equipment such as computers and desks, and how to inform customers and intermediaries.

While the mechanics of the implementation of the disaster plan was most impressive, by Monday morning all customer service staff were fully operational, the investment group was trading from new offices, electronic mail kept staff working from temporary offices informed, etc., the marketing and communication side was handled with the same skills.

By Saturday afternoon, less than 24 hours after the event, a press release was issued and advertising space was booked for Monday morning to inform customers and other concerned parties. On Sunday afternoon the switchboard was once again operational, enabling CU staff to respond to media enquiries. On Monday morning advertisements appeared in the national press confirming that it was 'business as usual' using the CU advertising theme 'We won't make a drama out of a crisis' in a highly appropriate and topical way.

The CU example shows that it is essential to be prepared for the unexpected. It also shows that even a major catastrophe such as the IRA bomb can be turned into an advantage provided plans are in place and management is aware of what to do. Crisis requires action and communication with key target groups. In order to do the right things the action plans need to be prepared in advance.

Who is in the target group?

This 'naive' question is raised as the answer is not as obvious as one would often like to think.

Originally target groups were defined along socio-economic criteria; a certain age, sex and income was as far as one could differentiate for practical purposes even though, conceptually, the thinking already went beyond this 20 years ago. Various psychological dimensions were sometimes incorporated in the creative development process but the use rarely extended further than that.

Appropriate targeting has always been important, with a more turbulent environment even more so. Change requires monitoring and the more specific one can be regarding the customer profile, the easier it becomes to define the group to monitor. Change occurs intermittently and at different speeds in different part of society, so a specific definition will decrease the risk of misunderstanding the customers.

The most serious misunderstanding in the traditional way of targeting is that it is assumed that people react the same way irrespective of product area. This is not true, a customer might well be a daring innovator in one respect and extremely conservative in another. Furthermore, it is not unusual that product requirements change with occasions. This is apparent in a business-to-business situation but is equally true in consumer goods. The criterion for a coffee to be consumed during the day is quite different from what is required as after-dinner coffee; a pint of lager on a sunny day in the garden has to deliver a different promise to a drink in a night club on a Friday night. Further examples have been published by A.C. Nielsen, the market research company; for instance, two out of every three buyers of low-fat yoghurt also buy luxury yoghurt, one in three diet cola buyers also buys the standard product. The individual is the same, different occasions generate different relationships to products.

Some of these pitfalls can be avoided by looking at 'user groups' rather than traditional target groups. The deeper understanding this requires will also take away some of the superficiality of the traditional groupings, still in frequent use in many companies.

Feedback loops

In previous chapters I have highlighted the importance of fast and accurate feedback loops. This is as important, or perhaps more important, when it comes to communication in relation to any other aspect of the marketing mix.

One aspect of this is that communication as such can have effects that are not the foreseen or intended; another is that an investment in communication via media is instant.

Once a message has gone out in the form of a commercial, there is no return. This is particularly true when we are dealing with television and radio commercials, but also newspaper advertisements, mailings and PR activities cannot be returned once published, sent out or released. An investment in a machine can partially be recovered if a project fails but once a commercial is on the air, the investment is gone for ever. Follow-up of activities to build up knowledge to optimize effectiveness is, of course, in such a situation very important. The feedback loops might not influence the campaign that is running at the moment of monitoring, but they can provide input for the next one.

Regarding the second aspect it is by no means certain that the target audience will react in the manner intended. As an illustration to this unpredictability I was once told the following story.

EXAMPLE 15.3

One day an inner-city teacher asked her class to write about the police. When she read the essays she was appalled by the hostility. One little boy just wrote one word: 'Bastards.'

To correct this attitude, the teacher and the police started a programme to familiarize the children with the police, having local police officers coming to the class, bringing in the police dogs, showing the police motorbikes, etc.

The teacher then set another essay with the same title, 'The Police'. This time the little boy wrote: 'Cunning Bastards.'

The unpredictability has several causes; one reason is that a message can be interpreted in many different ways due to different attitudes, backgrounds and social situations. Another is that the attitudes of the target audience tend to change, short term and long term. In the short term the effects of a television commercial can be influenced by the surrounding programme or even the other commercials in the break. In the longer term, attitudes do shift, and what is perfectly acceptable and interesting one year can be totally outdated the next.

The main reason why a message may be interpreted differently from what was intended is that the target group is made up of individuals with individual ways of reacting to messages.

For these reasons alone, it is essential with a system of feedback loops to read the market in a systematic or ad hoc way. A further reason is that the emerging new opportunities to communicate with the customers, via new types of media, make experimentation an important part of developing a strong future market position and, of course, there is no point in making experiments if one does not have systems in place to read and evaluate the new types of activities.

Summary

The more change we have in the marketplace, the more essential it becomes to have a communication strategy to ensure that the rate of change does not move away from dynamism to uncontrolled chaos, not forgetting the non-linear effects of communication inputs.

Message management and how to transfer the messages are two different issues and change within one aspect does not necessarily force change in the other. The successful communicators are those that ensure consistency across the media and develop the message gradually and dynamically in phase with, or slightly ahead of, the customers.

16

Branding: the communication short cut

The purpose of this chapter is to look at branding as it relates to chaos marketing and highlight a few aspects that are particularly relevant to marketers in a changing world.

During the 1980s the concept of the 'brand' took on an almost mythical role, fuelled by advertising agencies with vested interests in advertising spends and financial 'wizards' who saw brands as the justification for charging high prices for goods as well as companies.

The positive effect of this was that management realized that brands were valuable, the negative effect was that some managers drew the conclusion that the brand in itself was the essential factor, not the company behind it nor the product or service it represented.

The brand: the great communicator

A brand is never anything but a piece of communication. It simply is the name of a company, product or service. The brand identifies the producer, either directly as in the case of IBM or Heinz, or indirectly as in the case of Persil detergents or Johnny Walker whisky. The power of the brand lies in the reputation it represents.

As the brand is usually short and has a visual image as well as a name, conceptually it becomes a very efficient carrier of information and reputation, establishing the link between sender and recipient. It functions just like the name of a person. Names such as Margaret Thatcher or Mick Jagger evoke strong images because they represent much more than just the flesh and bones of an individual. In the commercial world the brand works the same way, identifying the 'bearer' and communicating to the world around us what the carrier of the brand has been up to in the past.

The real reason for the increasing importance of brands is exactly this aspect, the brand as an instant communicator. The time available for telling the potential customer what a product represents and what it stands for is getting increasingly shorter. With thousands of commercial messages being beamed at the public every day, each brand has a limited time available to tell its story. For consumer goods marketers the situation is even more pronounced in that just a visit to a supermarket will expose an individual to around 15 000 products with perhaps 1000 different brands and subbrands.

We can take the practical example of a commercial of 30 seconds. If the brand, on the screen for perhaps 5 seconds in total, can transfer values such as tradition, reliability, trustworthiness and value for money, the other 25 seconds can be spent on product features or endorsing a particular part of the brand's value mix. The economics of using the brand in the communication process becomes apparent.

When one considers the increasing number of messages surrounding and targeting all customer categories and the necessity to transplant quickly in the recipients' minds key value dimensions, the importance of branding becomes obvious.

The graphical execution, the design, of a brand has of course some relevance to this process: the easier it is to recognize a brand, the better. It is well worth noting, however, that it is not the visual identity as such that is of importance, it is the value dimensions the brand stands for that will determine whether the brand will function as an instant positive communicator or not.

To refer back to the two personalities mentioned above, it is unlikely that either Mick Jagger or Margaret Thatcher would have been well known if it had not been for what they have actually done. Just the visual impression and/or the name would not make much impact, as many aspiring rock 'n' roll singers and politicians well know. It is the reputation and, in marketing terms, the value that make a name a brand.

EXAMPLE 16.1

Leisure wear, and in particular trainers, is a market where marketers have 'indulged' in branding over the last decade. Inspired by the success of Reebok and Nike many other brands thought that just a name on an item would sell the product. Also, some of the more veteran brands thought they could follow in the slipstream of the leaders. The story of Puma, a major international sports goods brand, is an example of the fact that it is not that easy.

Puma has its roots in the German Dassler Bros., a family company founded in 1924 by two brothers Rudi and Adi Dassler. In 1948 the brothers split up; Rudi founded Puma and Adi founded Adidas. In-fighting between the two brothers' companies meant that Puma ignored the rise of Nike and Reebok, based on innovation and brand building, and in the early 1980s both Puma and Adidas lost market positions.

Puma, with traditional strengths in sports shoes, chose during the 1980s and early 1990s to copy Nike's marketing, with a focus on leisure rather than sport. The result was that whatever profile the brand had held previously soon disappeared and the advertising, according to observers, meant more to Nike than Puma.

It is only recently that Puma has gone back to concentrating on sports wear and, in particular, football boots, linking communication to the true roots of the brand rather than following the competitors. A brand does not create any competitive advantage when the profile, the reputation, is confusing and is only a conceptual me-too. The change to focus the Puma brand on what it actually stands for was long overdue: Puma lost around £8 million in 1993 on a turnover of around £170 million.

There is in many parts of the marketing profession a further misunderstanding of what the discipline of branding is actually all about, as indicated above.

This confusion has its roots in a mix up of graphical execution/ profile of a brand and branding as the communicator of values. Many companies have gone to great lengths to design a homogeneous and consistent graphical profile. Such an exercise is of very limited value unless the values are clear and communicated as a part of, or in tandem with, the graphical execution. Similarly, just a change of logo and/or any other branding device will not change customer perceptions in itself, perhaps apart from a short term 'aha' effect.

The new British Airways logo in the 1980s was an indication of a change in values, service and product and as such represented an excellent example of using graphical redesign as a signal of change. BP, the oil company, is in the author's view an example of the opposite. BP has a most consistent and beautifully executed corporate graphic design scheme but the brand itself does not represent distinct values, setting BP apart from the competitors.

The graphical execution is, of course, important but only if the values are clear to the recipients and the brand owners. The key to successful branding lies in connecting distinct and relevant value dimensions to the symbol or brand name.

Brand terminology

Another potentially confusing issue lies in the way brand
terminology is being used. Marketing studies often refer to regional,
national and international brands. This split is of course a true
reflection of the reality as seen from a brand owner's point of view,
but in most cases is totally irrelevant from the point of view of the
potential customers. For a customer all brands are local if they are
available; if not, the brand in question is of little interest. In smaller
countries there is an apparent fear of international brands. This fear
is unfounded from a conceptual point of view but, of course, is
highly relevant if the local brand is inferior in reputation (unlikely),
in product quality (possibly) and/or in marketing skills (quite
likely).

Another issue relates to the concept of private labels, i.e. retailers'
own labels. In the consumer goods industry there has been an on-
going debate for at least the last 20 years regarding own labels. The
success of Marks & Spencer's (virtually 100 per cent own label),
J Sainsbury's (60–70 per cent own label) and Tesco (around 50 per
cent own label) has encouraged a number of retailers to evaluate
this option and a number of manufacturers to reconsider their
strategies.

The conclusions of these strategy reviews have often been muddled
by a misunderstanding of the branding process, based on an
assumption that a retailer's brand on a product is different to a
product having a manufacturer's brand. If one considers the basics,
this assumption becomes quite absurd.

First, it is important to realize that own labels are not something
new. J Sainsbury's has had own labels for about 100 years and St
Michael of M&S was introduced in 1928. Many other quality
retailers, such as Harrods and Fortnum & Mason, have had own-
label goods virtually since their inception. Even Crosse & Blackwell,
Nestlé's grocery brand in the UK, has its origins in a retailing
organization.

Secondly, and more relevantly, the brand on a product denotes the
origins, regardless of what type of organization stands behind it. A
strong retailer with a good reputation will also have strong brand
values to go with the own-label products. The retailer's name on a
product will, for the same reasons, only work as long as the own-
label products are of good quality and provide value for money.

The only advantage an own-label product has over a manufacturer's
branded product is that the distribution is guaranteed. This can, of

course, be a significant factor but one should not neglect the fact that the distribution base is limited.

The semantics in branding can mislead the marketers. An own label is the same as another competitor, 'only' with an advantage in distribution; an international brand is no different from another brand, perhaps apart from a different marketing skills base.

Summary

Dynamic marketing environments and changing concepts can easily mislead a marketer. In the area of branding, the key issue remains the values behind the brand—in other words, the reputation the company has built up with the brand whether this has been done mainly via product quality as in the case of Marks & Spencer's, mainly via communication skills as in the case of Chanel perfume, or both as in the case of Levi's jeans. This reputation can have a fundamental impact on the ability of a company to influence a dynamic marketing system.

17

Advertising, media strategies and design

The communication discipline is often equated with advertising. This, of course, is not true but advertising remains the most discussed field in marketing and, alongside new product development, the area where one can most easily go from success to failure or vice versa as marginal differences can have fairly extreme effects.

It is also an area in which the chaos effects are quite clear and distinct. The stabilizing effects are as a rule pronounced, the nudge effect can be substantial and the possibilities and positive effects of feedback loops are perhaps greater than in many other fields.

The primary purpose of this chapter is to give some insight into how one can improve advertising effectiveness in a turbulent world. It is not the intention to give general guidelines on effective advertising or how to build strong brand values with advertising. The chapter also discusses other types of communication techniques and package design.

The communication high ground

Economies of scale

Advertising/communication is one of the factors in a company with the greatest potential from an 'economies of scale' point of view. The marginal cost of adding another 'viewer' to a commercial is zero and the opportunities to use creative materials across borders also improves the cost-effectiveness. This is of particular importance to brand leading companies in the consumer goods industries but is also relevant to other market sectors where advertising or some other type of communication either already forms a major part of the marketing mix or has the potential to become one. The way a product is produced is a totally different matter as one brand can cover many different product versions, particularly if the product executions are separated geographically.

The recession in the early 1990s in the UK has given rise to some conclusions on how advertising actually stabilizes and works to a brand leader's advantage. According to one study by Taylor Nelson AGB and the Billett Consultancy, FMCG companies that maintained or increased their advertising spend in the recession saw their market share increase. The study covered 127 brands and compared the first half of 1992 with the same period in 1991. The findings were that the best-performing brands had increased their spend by an average of 7 per cent and gained an average brand share of 1.1 per cent. The lowest-performing brands reduced their budget by 8 per cent and saw their share fall by 1.6 percentage points.

Another way of looking at the same situation is that the study also showed that the advertising to sales ratio of the 10 grocery product fields with the highest own-label share is less than 20 per cent of that for the 10 product fields with least own-label penetration. The brands that have invested in advertising have not suffered the same erosion of brand share to own label as has happened in sectors with less advertising.

It is difficult from this analysis to distinguish the effects of creative quality from pure media power. The probable truth is that it is a combination. It is unlikely that major successful advertisers have been spending money on commercials that are not reasonably effective, and it is also clear from the data that they have been spending considerable amounts.

The economies of scale in advertising makes it an interesting tool in marketing warfare. The main brand almost always has an advantage in media advertising as, assuming equal budgets and creative quality, the average cost per unit will be less than for the competitors while the sales effect will be at least the same or even higher due to a wider distribution base.

Share of voice vs share of market

Information published in an article in the *Harvard Business Review* in 1990 illustrates the economies of scale from another angle, by looking at the benefits of having a large market share. If a brand has, say, a market share of 30 per cent, the share of voice required to maintain that share is 25 per cent, i.e. 5 per cent less than the market share. If the market share is 10 per cent, the company needs a 14 per cent share of voice in order not to lose sales.

Another study published in the same journal provides a further dimension to the effects of share of voice versus share of market. The author of the second study, a vice-president of the consultants Booz, Allen & Hamilton, concluded that

> Market leaders win the ad spending war for market share by creating or exploiting disequilibrium and outspending their competitors by a wide margin for a sustained period. The study concluded that when a brand outspend another by 20–30 per cent then share change may well take place that can be correlated to adspend.

A significant spend is required to change the fairly stable customer behaviour, but once that has happened the new spending levels will create new market share positions, at a higher level for the leading brand.

The rationale for using advertising as a stabilizing factor is particularly strong for the brand leader. The reasons for maintaining a controllable dynamic development are much stronger than for a No. 2 and, of course, Nos 3 and 4 as there is more to lose and the economics are more positive, as illustrated above.

Message management

It was stated earlier that long-term success is more likely if one ensures that the message is consistent over time and does not deviate unnecessarily from previous campaigns (although, of course, dynamic development within the system is a necessity for long-term success). Potential technological changes in the media put extra pressure on this aspect.

Messages are often created from the standpoint of a specific type of media, sometimes deliberately, sometimes accidentally. It is, for instance, no accident that cigarette advertising messages are visually and graphically explicit as the restrictions on advertising limit the scope for copy-based messages and available media to outdoor and print. With an increasing supply of electronic as well as printed media, the transferability of messages across media within a limited time period becomes a competitive factor in itself.

EXAMPLE 17.1

Cigarette advertising used to be allowed in all forms of media but restrictions have gradually been introduced in most countries. Philip

Morris' Marlboro is an interesting example of 'message-management'—whether by design or accident is not clear to the author.

Initially Marlboro was launched in 1924 in the United States and positioned as a cigarette for women, with a red filter tip and the message 'a cherry tip for your ruby lips'. The brand was not a great success.

In 1955 the Marlboro brand was connected for the first time to the weather-beaten cowboy and Marlboro country. The positioning was changed totally to get as close as possible to Camel (endorsed by movie actors such as John Wayne), the then leading brand. The Marlboro country and cowboy image was introduced.

The first step of the message management was to change positioning to that of the leading competitor (the strong, outdoor, independent man) but in a more modern and perhaps more appealing execution.

When cigarette advertising was banned from radio and television in the United States, some brands had transitional problems but not Marlboro. The cowboy image could be enhanced as easily from outdoor or print as from television. The previous leading brand, Winston from R.J. Reynolds, did not succeed in transferring the message as well and lost the market leadership during the 1970s.

The second step of the message management was to transfer the message successfully from one type of media to another.

Lately, with increasing pressure on restricting tobacco advertising, Marlboro has moved into a more stylized message, using the colour red and the distinct graphical format from the pack to make the message even more independent of the type of media and changes to the media themselves.

The above illustrates how one can transfer a message from one type of media to another. Another aspect of the transferability of a copy platform is to adapt the message to the target audience, making the main message more relevant to customer groups by tailoring it to specific requirements.

EXAMPLE 17.2

In the early 1990s the Prudential Assurance Company creatively developed its main theme across media as well as target audiences. The starting point was television commercials with the line 'I want to be …'.

This copy line opened up opportunities for more specific targeting. One such example is that in the Educational supplement of the *Guardian* newspaper the headline of a Prudential advertisement read 'I want to be getting top marks for my pension', introducing to teachers the possibility of boosting their pension through the Prudential's additional voluntary contributions scheme.

The Prudential used variations of the theme, not only in consumer advertising. One headline was for an advertisement to recruit graduates to join the company: 'I want to be a high flyer.'

Another aspect of message management is the practice of using a commercial from one country in another. This is slowly gaining acceptance across Europe, mainly for no other reason than it saves costs and there is a comfort factor in that the chances are greater for a campaign to succeed if it has been tried somewhere else before, although this is by no means certain. From an 'export' point of view some messages, or executions, are more transportable than others. Themes such as family, children, home and security are universal, even though one might need to adjust the executions. On the other hand, humour, pets and to a degree sex are not nearly as easy to transfer from one country to another.

Although the marketing executive who restricts the creative process in order to make it potentially exportable is likely to make a mistake, it can be useful to bear the above in mind when considering transferring messages, and of course if a company is considering a multinational campaign from the start.

A message strategy that is comparatively rare but does open up interesting opportunities is to 'hijack' a potentially competing brand's advertising strategy (see also Chapter 10).

There are two situations in which this can be an operative alternative: one is when a company is challenging a brand leader, such as Marlboro in the case above; the other is when a company is taking pre-emptive measures to protect oneself from attacks of companies with multinational campaigns.

The first case is not unusual. A challenger adapts a strategy that is close to the brand leader's or takes the graphical values from a brand leader and uses that to enhance and classify one's own product. Colours are often used in such situations as they are rarely protectable. One such example is the frequent use of pink paper to denote financial information, hijacking *Financial Times* imagery. Another is to use 'Gold' to denote premium quality instant coffees, using the investment from Nescafé Gold Blend to boost one's own product.

As a short-term measure this can work quite well. In the medium term the execution has to be substantially better than the brand from which one is hijacking in order to be really successful; if not, the challenger will just not create any proprietary identity.

The second strategy, of adapting the creative strategy of an
international brand not yet on the market so that when the time
comes the international brand will not be able to use the
international campaign when launching, is not particularly common.
There are a few examples, some successful, others less so.

EXAMPLE 17.3

During the late 1980s I was involved in launching Findus Lean Cuisine
frozen prepared meals in Germany. Lean Cuisine had been a great
success in many countries—USA, UK, Sweden and France—but for
corporate reasons the brand had not been launched in Germany, nor
were any other Findus frozen foods products on the market in Germany.

In anticipation of the Findus launch, the main frozen food brand in
Germany, Unilever's Iglo, launched a range of similar products to Lean
Cuisine with a similar positioning, pack design and advertising under
the subbrand Delite.

At Findus our product range had thus to be modified to avoid
duplication with the brand leader and the design and advertising had
to be amended to create greater distinction to the 'domestic'
competitor.

The end result, several years later, was that both Delite and Lean Cuisine
stayed on the market; neither range was as successful as one would
have expected or planned and Iglo Delite was repositioned away from
Lean Cuisine after about one year. The Delite strategy was partly
successful in that it restricted the Lean Cuisine proposition and thus
perhaps reduced the sales, but it failed to stop the competitor.

The importance of having a message that can transfer across
different media was mentioned in the context of Marlboro. Another
aspect of the changing media scene is that changing technology and
regulations create new opportunities, especially for smaller
companies, to advertise and although they do not represent a threat
on a national level, in the local business environment the threat can
be real.

EXAMPLE 17.4

Cable television opens up opportunities for more effective
communication for smaller companies. One such example is Rob and
Tony Hore's carpet shop 'Discount Marketing' in Croydon, South
London.

With a production investment of £500 a commercial was created that
has had a dramatic effect, according to trade press sources. A media
cost of £12 per 30-second spot is also within the reach of most
companies. The television commercials have been successful because,
compared to the traditional press advertisements, the television

medium makes it possible to have a more personal presentation of the individuals in the store, the products are better presented and, in this case, the media has been used to its advantage in that a media personality has been created.

Summary

Advertising has long been regarded as the apex of the marketing pyramid. It is exciting, it has glamour and if you do it right the rewards are significant. From a chaos marketing point of view advertising can be used to great effect in managing, or more accurately influencing, the market dynamics through building a *sustainable* competitive advantage.

Media strategies and tactics

The media industry in most parts of the world has been exposed to a fair amount of change over recent years. The communication revolution, the development of cable television, the prospect of various interactive media programmes and many other developments have changed and will continue to change the media market.

To operate in this environment successfully one has to take a different view of the way a message is transmitted from the way it is created and perceived. While the above has indicated that at least a certain amount of conservatism in the message management is advisable, the media's technological changes have to be taken into the management process sooner rather than later, and proactively rather than reactively. As in the case of Marlboro, the message can stay the same even if the media is changing.

Media planning, i.e. how to buy advertising space, is an art in itself and the purpose of this short section is only to highlight a few aspects that are of particular relevance from a general marketing management point of view.

Global strategy, local implementation

A more offensive use of the media-buying function can have interesting effects and conclusions. A study quoted earlier in the chapter concluded that with significant relatively higher spend, the system could be turned to the brand leader's advantage. Looking at such a suggestion on a national scale might well prove to be discouraging as the financial implication might be substantial as it is necessary to apply the higher levels of spend for a significant time, at least a couple of years.

The proposed suggestion is to apply the 'global' strategy in a regional or local way. By selecting the most appropriate regions— i.e. where it would be easiest to outspend the main rivals—and investing on a region by region basis, the company can make the easiest victories first. Funds can be generated to pay for a more aggressive stance in the more 'expensive' regions and thus gradually roll over the competitor in a cost-effective and long-term way.

It should, of course, be noted that the strategy is unlikely to work unless the company has a cost leadership in the structure, otherwise it can itself be outspent by the competitors and all will be lost.

So the first conclusion is to be regional, or local, in the approach to media buying. It is always worth remembering, as in the case of branding, that all business is local; the total national success is built from singular decisions by individuals and it is the frames of mind of these individuals that determine the level of success, in consumer and industrial goods.

Media proliferation

Another aspect of the changing media world is the rise of new types of media and more variants within many existing media formats.

New types of media open up new channels with different opportunities and restrictions. For instance, fax magazines and the, by now, almost old-fashioned teletext increase the speed of communication. At the same time we have seen a decline in the traditional general women's magazines in most parts of Europe. The media buyer obviously has to be aware of these changes, use the media where appropriate and include them in a schedule only when they fulfil the criteria.

New media does not only occur in the 'modern' Western world.

EXAMPLE 17.5

The first truly democratic election in South Africa caused a few interesting observations from a media point of view. The diverse population of South Africa, plus the exclusion of main media such as television, meant that the advertising agencies advising the political parties had to find other ways of reaching the mass audiences.

Community newspapers formed one non-traditional media, with circulation numbers going from almost nothing to 50 000. Bill boards formed another route: the use of visual imageries rather than the printed word was in any case a more effective communication method owing to the high levels of illiteracy. Among the more unusual media listed was StarTaxiMusic, a company that supplies free music tapes with intermittent ads to the large bus taxi industry. Another way of reaching the rural part of the population was a video road show, taking a high-tech approach to a low-tech environment.

The main concern, though, for most media buyers is the fragmentation of the market. This is particularly relevant in consumer goods as this is the sector with the largest media budgets and where, perhaps, the effects of fragmentation are likely to be the largest.

A study by Ogilvy & Mather in 1992 showed conclusively, and perhaps not surprisingly, that media fragmentation leads to a slower pace of building net cover and a more concentrated impact distribution towards the higher end of the scale. In lay terms, a company would need to buy more spots to reach the same number of viewers and the short-fall would be among the light viewers. The heavy viewers would still see the commercial as often as in a non-fragmented market.

In practical terms it used to be possible in the UK to reach up to 65 per cent of housewives with one spot; but currently the best anyone can hope for is around 40 per cent and in the United States the highest rating is around 20 per cent. In a truly segmented market this would not be much of a problem, but most of the changes in broadcasting, especially television, have led to similarity in offers, which is why there is fragmentation rather than segmentation.

The necessity of attention to detail in buying media becomes even more crucial in such a scenario. The smaller audiences per viewing makes mistakes more likely. There is a greater risk of duplicating audiences when buying many small audiences than if you buy large chunks per spot. In the latter case you cannot have duplication as each extra viewer is just that, contrary to buying the same number of viewers at different occasions.

The second conclusion is that fragmented media means that more money will be required to achieve the same results, everything else being equal. As a secondary effect, the attention to detail becomes even more important and the risk of making mistakes increases.

The fragmented media scene with greater multiplicity of types of media bring about temptations to spread one's budget across many different types of communication channels. This temptation must be avoided as experience, as well as theory, favours a policy of media dominance. Although overkill in the amount of money spent in one channel is not efficient, it is equally true that relatively small amounts are inefficient. If a brand is to be brand leader it needs to allocate funds accordingly, and, as a rule, if a challenger is to be noticed the threshold for getting noticed is fairly high. In particular, if the strategy is one of stabilizing a system the local market media needs to be dominated.

Summary

To buy media is a very important function for many companies. In a turbulent world it requires a more local approach to buying the media—not to be confused with the creation of advertisements—and an even more alert approach to getting the best deal in purchasing advertising space in a fragmented market.

Other types of media

Advertising is the most discussed part of the communication mix, but many other methods exist to reach the potential customers, such as direct communication, PR, word-of-mouth and personal selling.

The main principles are similar to those that apply to advertising but the character of each of these disciplines opens up some interesting perspectives.

Direct communication

More commonly known as direct mail, this is probably the communication method that has gone through the greatest amount of change recently and where even more change is expected in the future. Many of the technological opportunities appearing from the electronic world have applications in this field.

Better targeting from the sender's point of view, more opportunities to customize the message and, perhaps above all, greater possibilities to respond represent just a few factors. For instance, the possibilities opened up by desktop publishing represent a quiet revolution. Brochure layouts that took days to alter in the not-too-distant past can now be changed in seconds.

It should also be noted that direct communication is really the only proper 'mechanical' method for 'real' communication. Communication implies a dialogue, not a monologue, and it is only the personally addressed communication with encouragement to and possibilities for a response that really lives up to the term 'communicating' with the respondent.

If a company can build a real relationship with the customers with the help of databases, etc., that relationship can be a very strong bond and one that is unlikely to be unsettled by challenging companies. A properly run direct communication system is very stable, as can be seen from the relative stability, and profitability, of many such companies, such as the *Reader's Digest*.

These factors, together with the possibilities for faster feedback loops than traditional advertising, makes the medium well worth exploring for many companies.

I would like to add one personal word of caution. The feeling of togetherness that the direct communication can establish between the company and the customer is sometimes devalued by a lack of apparent social acceptance. The fact that a message is displayed privately, rather than publicly, can influence the general acceptability of a message.

Public relations

Public relations, or PR, is another aspect of how to deal with the customers, how to disseminate information and build loyalty.

PR can be extremely cost-effective or wasteful, because it deals with elements of the marketing system that are less controllable. Essentially, PR uses the previously described multiplier-effect in that a message, a 'push', is sent out and depending on the environment in which it lands (metaphorically speaking) the effect can be either very positive or none at all. Dealing with the public in this indirect way does mean that it is essential to have feedback loops that are sensitive to changes in the target audience. It is equally important to have an organizational set-up that can act quickly, either proactively when there is good news or reactively when something negative is happening.

EXAMPLE 17.6

During the late 1980s aerobics became fashionable in the UK with a great number of participants. A number of commercial activities flourished along with this interest, such as the publication of a number of exercise videos, some based on aerobics experts, other featuring well-known (and beautiful) celebrities. During early 1994 signs of waning interest started to show; for instance, new issues of celebrity videos were not showing the sales successes of previous years.

For 1994, Flora, Unilever's margarine spread, decided to sponsor the 1994 Aerobathon, an aerobics event in six locations across the UK, expecting 140 000 participants, and raising £3 million for charity. The intention was to build on the success of the 1993 Aerobathon which, without any significant marketing support, managed to attract 26 000 people to one venue in London. With marketing support from Flora, such as on-pack information and a TV campaign, the sights were set higher.

According to press reports the result was that only 17 000 people showed up, the raised money did not even cover the costs and the charities received no contributions.

The sponsorship was not a success for Flora, no goodwill was generated and perhaps even some 'badwill' resulted from the project. The conclusion from the angle of using PR in a changing world is that one must have very sensitive feedback loops to monitor the marketplace. The warning signals were either not picked up or ignored with an unsatisfactory end result.

The reasons for the financial failure of the above event are outside of the scope of this book. However, a more cost-effective way of using PR is illustrated in the following example.

EXAMPLE 17.7

The Gillette launch of Sensor for Women was different from the usual high-profile activity of an FMCG giant. The launch programme was built around the fact that a shaver for women is a much more personal product than a shaver for men.

The PR activities included visits by the designer and brand manager to the beauty editors of women's magazines to ensure that the influential editors knew of the product. The company, or its PR agency, also released interesting social trends on shaving, results from an omnibus survey on what men and women thought represented a 'good pair' of legs (with appropriate illustrations), plus the usual samples, competitions and so on. The result was that within three months of the launch the product had captured 40 per cent of all razor sales.

PR correctly applied to the marketplace can have quite extraordinary effects; if it is done wrongly the whole exercise will be totally wasted, even more so than in the case of advertising. PR is also, by definition, a public activity, likely to create positive and negative feelings beyond the narrow group of product users.

Word-of-mouth

Word-of-mouth is an activity closely related to PR, and sometimes integrated with it. The chaos system opens up opportunities to 'manipulate' the public to talk about products and services. Many products play an important role in the lives of the public and if those products can initiate a topic of conversation at the dinner table, in the pub or on the bus going home from work, immediately a communication effect is taking place.

This effect can, of course, be both negative and positive. Unfortunately the negative effects tend to spread at least twice as fast as the positive ones, so great care has to be taken to ensure that the 'campaigns' that are started are positively positive.

Successful campaigns in this area depend on a very keen awareness of what the customers think and feel regarding the product. To field the right issues via PR, advertising, direct mail shots or whatever media is available is a necessity for success, but with the right multiplier effect a small investment can pay immediate dividends.

The technique is often used by restaurants to create a local point of difference. Even on a large scale it can work: one of London's most famous restaurants in volume terms, the Hard Rock Café, depends totally on word-of-mouth for communicating and building brand image.

Word-of-mouth is probably the cheapest form of targeted communication. It is truly unreliable with a very strong non-linear effect. The very format makes it impossible to control but if a company has the right sensitivity to the market a small investment in creativity can create a lot of positive impressions.

Personal selling

Personal selling is mentioned in this context in order to ensure that it is not forgotten. It is a traditional way of working. It is impossible to cover the subject in any detail within the context of this book and it remains a most powerful tool when correctly used, despite technological progress.

The personal dialogue is potentially the strongest form of communication; consequently it is also the best way of creating a dominating position in the minds of the customers. From this it follows that it can have a significant stabilizing influence in a turbulent market, with a few provisos.

The personal relationships that many salespersons have with customers are only worth something for the company if that relationship is tied directly to the company, rather than just to the individual. So the short-term 'agent' type of sales representation is not likely to be as beneficial in the long term as a dedicated salesforce.

Another consequence is that personal selling in a changing world will only work if it is consistent with the company's overall business objectives. The salesforce has to be totally in tune with the company's overall strategies and tactics. This requires fast communication, far superior to older types of sales bulletins, so that the sales operation is in harmony with the company's main activities.

The salesforce of a company is, or should be, an important part of the feedback systems. The sales representatives are seeing customers and the response and information they receive must be channelled back as quickly, as accurately and as comprehensively as possible.

Summary

Communication is not only about advertising, the reality for most brands and companies is that non-advertising communication programmes are more important. The opportunity to use new technology is tempting and can be put to good use, but the message management must follow the rules of good communication in order to fulfil the stabilizing role in the dynamics of the marketing system.

Product and pack design

Pack design, particularly in the FMCG markets, is of fundamental importance. It is the most cost-effective way of communicating with the customers and it is also the one that gives the ultimate benefits of scale; a pack design for one million packs costs the same as for one single pack.

What follows is very much written with FMCG products in mind, but at least some of the reasonings and conclusions also apply to other market sectors.

The importance of pack design was highlighted by a statement from the 3rd UK Design Effectiveness Awards: 'For every penny that retailer Boots spent on new packaging designs for its own-label hosiery, it gained £1 in sales.'

Pack design development used to be something that was cast in stone. One design execution was expected to last many years without change. The advent of more effective design tools, more flexibility in manufacturing and, of course, greater awareness of the potentials have meant that the 'life-time' of one specific design solution has shortened.

The dynamics of this process must be managed with skill in that development is necessary to avoid stagnation, but the main messages and the overall familiarity must not be lost. Depending on market position and, of course, market sector the dynamics differ; a strong brand leader needs to develop with great care, any upcoming new product design needs to move forward while not alienating the customers already converted to the brand. Brands such as Nescafé, Kellogg's, Kit-Kat, etc., do not change dramatically over night. The design is changed gradually so that the familiarity and recognition are maintained—which is very important in a turbulent world.

The other angle of the renewal process is customizing. The closer to a customer's requirements a product can be designed, the more likely it is that the customer will remain loyal (assuming everything else is equal). The customizing process can involve all kinds of dimensions—everything from engraving something with a name to designing something totally unique for a specific customer. Provided that the customizing process keeps to the variables that can be changed without the company losing its identity, it will build loyalty; if it goes so far that the company's identity disappears, the loyalty will also disappear.

Design is also a discipline in which the details are of great importance. The space available on a pack is restricted and how it is used can make the difference between success and failure.

EXAMPLE 17.8

Matey has been the brand leader in children's bathcare products for about 30 years. The market changed during the early 1990s: from 1990 to 1992 the retail market more than doubled to £10 million due to new product activity, mainly in the form of bubble bath containers in the shape of licensed cartoon characters such as Ninja Turtles. This change to the marketplace made Matey's position less strong. Its old packs were less colourful and did not have the same play value. The competition had destabilized the market with new product activity.

In spring 1993 Matey launched a new range with new, proprietary, characters on the bottles and the bottles themselves were redesigned with new shapes and colours. The result was that sales increased dramatically, growing from 27 per cent of the market to around 50 per cent by the end of 1993.

The pack design is in a sense a larger version of a company's logo. It is by looking at the pack design that the customers will recognize a product. The messages that are incorporated in the design are essential to a product's perception and those messages need to be communicated consistently to the customers. So it follows that the main message in a design is something that should be changed only gradually and with care and consideration for the past history of the product, maintaining and strengthening the link with the customers.

It is equally true that to stand still is to fall behind. As the customers change, the products need to change—unless, of course, the company or the brand represents total tradition when no change might well be the most clever route to communication.

To challenge, a company can adapt different strategies. One very common strategy is to copy the brand leader as far as possible and hope to 'steal' sales that way, by hijacking a design. The other alternative is to go far away from the existing product design, break new ground and build a 'self-made' profile. The former is the safer route but as any copy is unlikely to move beyond being just that, it is not an easy way to become brand leader and the efficiencies of the strategy lie in gaining short-term acceptance. The latter has greater possibilities in the long term but more risks short term. Both alternatives are commonly followed, which route will be best in an individual case depends on the circumstances.

Pack and product design is the primary communication tool in many cases; 'proper' advertising campaigns are only available to a minority of brands. It is relatively cheap and the effects of doing it well can be dramatic. From a management point of view, the element of change has to be managed with care, depending on market position.

Conclusions

Advertising and other communication tools opens up great opportunities to build long-term loyalties and thus stabilize the marketing system in favour of the proactive communicator and/or to create sufficient barriers to challengers.

The element of dynamic development is a necessity, as is the understanding that media and message should follow different strategies, especially in a turbulent world.

18
Management: battling with the unknown

Good strategies and tactics are a function of good management, and good management is necessary to implement well-developed strategies and tactics, a circular argument that is putting the spotlight on the importance of good management.

From a marketing point of view, one has to look at the management process from two angles: on the one hand, how do you manage the marketing function and, on the other, how does the company deal with marketing issues? The following is mainly regarding the former although at the end of the chapter a few general management issues, together with an evaluational check-list, are included. It is my view that it is of greater importance for a company to look at 'how to do it' and 'what to do' rather than 'who should do it'.

The organizational issues cannot, however, be ignored; for instance, the way a company is organized does influence working patterns. Considering the element of change, the generally unsettled nature of marketing executives and the debate regarding the effectiveness of the marketing function it is not surprising that the future of the marketing departments has been debated fairly extensively over the last 10–15 years. The discussions have resulted in limited actual change, although the author will be making a few suggestions and indicating some trends below.

The 'turbulent' organization

It is almost self-evident that an organization that is acting within a turbulent environment has to be flexible and has to be prepared to deal with the unforeseen. It is therefore essential that the organizational structure is also flexible in its ability to adapt to change, or even use change to its advantage. It is not necessary, however, for an organization to continually reorganize in order to be successful, and it is certainly not an advantage if the staff are changing as well as the marketplace.

A system that is well-organized and in place has a much greater ability to adapt to change and assimilate ideas than one that is in itself in turmoil. As a comparison, a healthy biological system can absorb a certain amount of pollution with little or no side-effects while an unbalanced system will not be able to cope with even limited outside effects. Similarly, if the established structure does not take into account the changes and adapt to them, the ability to absorb and even use change diminishes over time.

Constant evolution in the way a company and, in particular, the marketing and sales departments are managed is the most favoured route for coping with change and ensuring that the company can manage the unforeseen.

At the core of this assumption lies the fact that it is not organizations as such that manage and execute, it is individuals but the individuals need to be in an environment which allows them to contend with change. Usually the ones most able to identify change and who know instantly what to do are those who have experience and knowledge of the marketplace. If you do not know the background it is very difficult to make an accurate assessment of competitive activity, to understand customers' responses and to know what to do immediately to achieve the best results.

In the author's view many marketing departments are mismanaged from this point of view. During the 1980s, but also more recently, the focus in marketing recruitment has been on creativity, to find new angles. Surveys have shown that the average time spent by brand managers on a brand has been as short as 18 months, and even marketing directors change on average after three years. As one advertising agency executive in London remarked: 'We have a situation where the undisciplined are leading the untutored.'

If marketing departments are staffed by executives with limited knowledge of a market, it is of course unlikely that they will have the knowledge required to make fast and accurate decisions—which is necessary in a changing world. This is one of the many dichotomies of marketing for the future: stability in the executional part makes an organization more adept to deal with change. It has to be added, with force, that this is only true if the 'stable' organization is open to change, is aware of what is happening and is prepared to use its abilities to force the company to make changes appropriate to the market situation. It should also be clear that the term 'stability' refers to the individuals, not the organizational format that needs to follow, or even pre-empt, developments in the marketplace.

From a personal view I would like to add that the marketing executives are likely to be more effective and produce better results if they are really committed to their products and enjoy what they are doing. As the novelist Colette allegedly advised a son wanting to wed: 'Beware of girls who do not like wine, truffles, cheese or music.'

As indicated above, the formal organogram of a marketing department is of less importance than the way the individuals act or their professionals skills. Despite this, the subject requires a few comments.

Over the last few of years the brand management system has been criticized in many ways; for instance, Unilever's co-chairman Floris Maljers indicated in 1992 in *Marketing* magazine that 'the halcyon days of brand management are over'.

The main concern among marketing directors and general managers is the apparent limited productivity of marketing departments. A further reason for concern is that the responsibilities of the marketers can not only differ from one division of a company to another, the formal responsibility is often not consistent with the real one. Furthermore, the roles of the marketers are multi-fold; there is the evangelical role of being the customers' main spokesperson in the company, driving the company towards customer orientation, and there are functional responsibilities such as developing products, advertising and promotional campaigns.

These general concerns have to be coupled with the changes brought about by the marketplace with demands on greater professionalism. Although it is unlikely that the same solution will be appropriate for different companies, two alternative development routes are indicated below. In both instances it is my belief that the evangelical role of ensuring or making a company marketing oriented should be vested with the CEO or possibly the marketing director. It is not the role of brand managers, or even marketing managers, to do this; it is a company strategy that has to be advocated from the top. Accepting this reduction of the marketing department's mission the task becomes one of ensuring the best professional standards and the greatest ability to adapt to and act in a turbulent world.

The first alternative is to organize along functional lines, i.e. rather than having brand managers being 'Jacks of all trades and masters of none', executives would be advertising managers, promotions managers, product development managers, etc., with a brand supremo coordinating and inspiring the total activity package. Some companies already follow this pattern—at least partly—in that they buy in marketing services from functional specialists, retaining only a core marketing function within the company.

The second alternative, which at the time of writing appears to be the more popular, is to have the executives' positions aligned with the customer structures. In this system the executives remain 'Jack of all trades' but by specializing in customer sectors they develop much greater understanding of the special requirements needed. Also in this case a 'supremo' is needed to coordinate the total package.

EXAMPLE 18.1

A mix of the two principles was behind organizational change in Unilever's Elida Gibbs in 1993. The post of brand manager was abolished, as was the sales department. The brand management function was renamed brand development managers, charged with pulling together product innovation and technical and management resources focusing on the consumers. The sales role has been taken over by customer development managers, responsible not only for sales but also total category management.

The above has been very much related to the human aspect of responding to and using change. Obviously technical solutions, especially in computer technology, have made it possible for organizations to improve their competitiveness. Personal computers in particular, but also information technology in a wider sense, have transformed many tasks and routines.

Planning

Creating marketing plans has been a key part of the marketing executive's job description for a long time. Many companies have a budget cycle of a long-term plan covering 3–6 years plus an annual budget detailing Year 1 of the plan. These plans are usually created and decided upon, at least in principle, six months before the end of the accounting year; in other words, the lead time from decision to the last execution of the operational plan is around 18 months. While the yearly plans used to be obsolete after a few months, in many sectors they are now obsolete almost before they have been printed.

The initial chapters on how to adapt to a changing marketplace illustrated the importance of planning 'how' to do things but to keep the execution on hold for as long as possible. Marketing planning obviously has to adapt to this as well. The only plans that have a reason for their existence are those that focus on understanding the customers, those that focus on how to implement and those that prepare for the unknown by looking at alternatives.

To be a workable document a marketing plan needs to be adaptable, and the creators of the document must have an understanding of the implications of change to the plans and which activities can be committed early and which can be left until later. It is also, of course, important to have an expressed view of how to influence the marketing system—for instance, whether the objective is to create stability or turbulence, and which tools to use to achieve this.

One also needs to question the yearly planning cycle. It is a practical tool for seasonal products and it happens to tie in with the accounting practices. In most areas that is rapidly becoming too slow a process, and why should the competitive environment follow the pattern of the earth's seasons?

The yearly pattern is often defended by the need, at least once a year, to have a thorough review of a brand's position. Although this is a valid point it is not an excuse for retaining a planning cycle that is much too long for the modern world. How short the planning cycle should be is a function of each particular industry, but a generalization for a 'normal' company would be to operate on a quarterly basis with a constant rolling forward of 12 months' planning because some activities still require that kind of lead time.

The quality of the thinking in the plan is, of course, what will determine whether a plan will generate success or not. It is important to show independence in thought and to consider the facts, not from the prevailing wisdom's point of view but from a realistic perspective of the business.

EXAMPLE 18.2

When the chief executive of the Prudential Insurance Company, Mr Keith Bedell-Pearce, presented his thoughts on marketing at the UK Marketing Society's annual conference in 1992 he stressed the importance of 'bucking the trend'.

When the Prudential followed the general trend in the 1980s to diversify into estate agents, the result was disastrous and the decision by Mr Bedell-Pearce was 'to get out quick'.

On a positive and more current note the Pru also bucked the trend when it decided to get into the personal pension market. The general view was that the market would be around 0.5 million individuals. The Prudential thought otherwise and estimated the market to be 5 million. At the time of the speech, the Prudential had already sold more than 500 000 pensions.

It pays to look carefully at how one's product is really perceived and where the best potential lies for sales. The common view might not necessarily be the correct one as the previous and following examples illustrate.

EXAMPLE 18.3

Avon is known worldwide for its cosmetics and the home selling technique, the 'Avon Lady'. Avon grew dramatically during the 1950–70s but in the 1980s sales started to dwindle in the home market in the United States. As a consequence, Avon started to expand abroad in a more aggressive and creative manner.

Latin America now accounts for more than one-third of world sales, Brazil being the biggest market with a turnover of over $500 million in 1993 and a salesforce of 320 000. Of these 60 000 form the Amazon salesforce, travelling by foot, kayak, riverboat and plane to find new and existing customers.

In the gold-mining town of Patrocino, according to the *Sunday Times*, flexibility is the key to success: 'Two dozens of eggs buys a Bart Simpson deodorant. 20 lb of flour gets a Misty cologne and a four gram gold nugget buys a bottle of fragrance such as Sweet Crystal Splash, which normally retails for $9.'

No economic indicators would have told Avon that this part of the world would be perfect for the Avon system. As the president of Avon Brazil said: 'The economists thought we were crazy to go to places like Patrocino. They are right if you look at the economic indicators, because there aren't any.'

One way of examining whether a process is necessary or not is to look at the success rate of those that follow it and those that don't. A study of 2994 start-ups was made in the US in 1990 by the National Federation of Independent Business in order to evaluate the importance of planning. The result was that

> the founders who spent a long time in study, reflection and planning were not more likely to survive their first three years than people who seized opportunities without planning. In fact many corporations that

revere comprehensive analysis develop a refined incapacity for seizing opportunities.

Another study of 100 of the fastest growing 500 companies in the US showed that 41 per cent had no business plan at all, 26 per cent had just a very simple 'back-of-an-envelope' plan, 5 per cent worked out financial projections for investors and 28 per cent wrote a proper full plan. (Both studies published in the *Harvard Business Review*.)

This does not, however, imply that the successful entrepreneurs succeeded without any planning at all. What they had was an intuitive ability to analyse plus the ability to screen opportunities quickly, to focus on the key issues and to integrate action and analysis—that is, be ready to change course.

This shows that it is essential to have a way of working which constantly evolves, develops and adapts to change and systems which ensure that there is constant feedback. Formal and informal feedback loops are essential, and they need to be fast!

Budgeting

Today, hardly any company operates without a budget. Some companies have detailed systems, others less so. From a marketing point of view, budgets are dealt with from at least two different angles: on the one hand there are sales budgets or sales targets, and on the other there are cost budgets, i.e. limits to what one department or function can spend.

The concept of budgeting assumes a stable environment and that one can foresee what is going to happen within the horizon of the budget. That was rarely true in the past and is even less so now.

The need for budgeting has further declined because modern computer technology can deal with accountancy information much more quickly than previously. In the past, when calculations were made by hand, it was necessary to have predetermined criteria with which to evaluate the performance, whether from a revenue or cost point of view. A detailed budget fulfilled that role.

Today, and even more in the future, a company can have all data 'on-line' and know the *actual* cost of the product as soon as it has left the factory floor, or even before. The implications of this is that the main criteria for the business still need to be clearly defined and budgeted, but in the case of the specifics the reality is a much better yardstick than any predetermined budget.

The 'only' time a budget in the classical sense is required is when a company has decided to make an exceptional investment. In order to evaluate whether the investment is viable or not one needs to do some calculations, and the profit criteria need to be amended to allow for the extra fixed costs that need to be covered. Similarly, the cash flow plan needs to be amended to allow for extra expenditure.

A move from budget focus to on-line actual cost and revenue awareness will provide better and more accurate information and make the organization more aware of what is happening at the present, improving the quality of the feedback loop.

For the sales budget the same reasoning applies. Reaching a budgeted figure is in itself a non-event. It is only when the relative market position of a company has improved—with a positive cost/revenue result—that sales and marketing executives have reason to celebrate.

If cost and revenue information is quicker at hand with faster feedback loops, the marketers can also take remedial and/or aggressive action much more quickly and with better knowledge than in the past, all to the benefit of the corporation.

The way most companies budget the marketing expenditures and sales forecasts is almost antiquated. Faster feedback loops measuring the real development and the actual financial situation in combination with simplistic key profit targets ($£x$/unit or x per cent of customer y's purchases) will free management time from budgeting to ensuring that the company is moving forward and gaining competitive advantages.

Battle strategies and tactics

Chaos marketing is about finding ways of surviving and winning the marketing battle; general management advice is not really part of the 'brief'. The following paragraphs present reflections seen from the perspective of marketing management; they are based on what appears to be the right way to operate in order to be profitable, putting an additional perspective on the previous.

It has been mentioned that it is essential for an organization to be dynamic and adaptable in order to be sufficiently effective in a changing business environment. One part of ensuring that the organization remains flexible and open to outside influence is to recognize, and even encourage, dissent and conflict. One of the most successful professional managers of all times, Alfred Sloan of General Motors, expressed in his *My Years with General Motors* that dissent and conflict are necessary and even desirable because without them there will be no understanding, and understanding is necessary for making the right decisions.

In the previously quoted *Harvard Business Review* article on successful entrepreneurs, the authors concluded that 'profitable survival requires an edge derived from some combination of a creative idea and a superior capacity for execution'.

Although the quote referred to rapidly growing companies, the conclusion is also of value to more established companies. The ability to execute efficiently and effectively is a recurring theme when looking at successful operations.

When a company operates in a rapidly changing environment, one can easily draw the conclusion that it is essential to constantly invent in order to stay ahead. This is a misconception; it is necessary to *innovate*, but not to *invent*. Companies strong in inventing such as Philips in Holland are usually not as strong as those with the ability to innovate, such as Sony of Japan.

Many of the most successful companies are built around a strong executional tradition. Successes such as McDonald's, IKEA, Benetton and Kellogg's are based on excellent executional disciplines. These companies/brands also constantly innovate in order to improve the product or service; they are never satisfied, always strive for improvement, but rarely have any real breakthrough inventions.

The other part of the execution-oriented strategy is to be open for opportunities and exploit them. Microsoft was built, for example, not on a breakthrough product but on the ability to exploit the opportunity that IBM offered with the PC operation system, later called MS-DOS.

Change is really the friend of the successful and alert company. The managers who reminisce on a time when there was less change not only miss an opportunity to develop and create something new, but they fundamentally misunderstand the reality.

Change opens up new opportunities for growth and profits which is to the alert company's advantage: instead of having to spend resources to fight them, the market forces will take care of any 'sleeping' competitors. Change also unleashes powerful resources in the market which a company can use to its advantage, either by identifying and using the trends or proactively influencing the trends in a more favourable direction. It is easier to readjust a moving object than to get it rolling in the first place.

It is only when change gets out of control that it can be to the detriment of a company. It is worth noting that it might be possible to stabilize a rapidly changing system, but a system that is totally out of control is really just that: uncontrollable. From a management point of view one has to put this into perspective and realize that it rarely happens and that most companies have tools within their power that they can use to defuse a possible 'eruption'.

From a general standpoint a dynamic chaos market system is to be preferred, especially when management is aware of how to manage change to the company's advantage.

Summary

To summarize from a chaos marketing management point of view the key issues are:

- Understand the marketplace and the dynamics of constant evolution.
- Don't be afraid of change. Use it and change with it.
- Prepare mentally for the unexpected.
- Build strengths and relationships.
- Plan how to do it, and implement as late as possible.
- Act decisively when required.
- Empower the individual. Remember that all departments and target groups depend on individual decision making.

And finally, a marketing or sales manager or any other executive in a (democratic) society can only influence. Never believe that you can control a market or a customer group, that is an illusion.

Do you live in a turbulent world?

The perceptions of an individual executive are easily flavoured by short-term events and comments made in the general and trade media. The question of whether a particular market sector is in 'turmoil' or not, whether it is likely to move into an uncontrollable phase, or whether it is about to stagnate is not always easy to determine.

The check-list below has been developed to give some guidance in evaluating the real and potential rate of change and on how a company is positioned. The intention is not that the list in itself will provide a score, although if you evaluate a sufficient number of sectors you will get a 'branch index', but to highlight the areas which influence the rate of change. The comparison between the company/brand and the market will, however, give some indications as to how dynamic the company is, how well equipped it is to manage change and how likely it is that the market position will change.

The list has been developed with a manufacturing consumer goods company in mind but can easily be amended to suit any company whether in the consumer or industrial goods sector and whether the company is in the service or manufacturing industry.

Evaluational check-list

Market assessment

Market development, ± per cent
     Volume: ....
     Value: ....

Average age, top five brands:.....
Accumulated change in brand
     shares:.............................
No. of new brands last two
     years: ....
Customer loyalty: ....

Average age, top 20
     products:.........................
Accumulated change top five
     products:.........................
No. of new products last three
     years: ....
No. of new products last year: ....
No. of product innovations last
     year:.............................

Share integrated distribution to
     customer: ....
Share change in distribution
     method last two years:........
Share of customers visited by
     sales reps:........................
Marketing mix:
     Share spent on
     communication: ....
     Share spent on price
     promotion:.......................
Share of sales with price
     promotion:.......................
Degree of price changes last 12
     months: ....

Company assessment

Sales development, ± per cent
     Volume: ....
     Value: ....
Market share:........................

Average age top three
brands: ....

Accumulated change in
brand shares:......................

No. of new brands last two
years:................................

Brand loyalty: ....

Average age top 10 products:....

Accumulated change top three
products: ....

No. of new products last three
years:................................

No. of new products last year:.....

No. of product innovations last
year: ....

Share integrated distribution to
customer:............................

Share change in distribution
method last two years:.........

Share of customers visited by
sales reps: ....

Marketing mix:
  Share spent on
  communication:..................

  Share of voice:.......................

  Share spent on price
  promotion: ....

Share of sales with price
promotion: ....

Degree of price changes last 12
months:..............................

Summary

Total market: ....

Degree of volatility:....................

....

  Main reasons: ....

....

Trend: ....

....

Indices: ....

....

Company:...................................

Degree of brand volatility: ....

....

  Main reasons: ....

....

Trend: ....

....

Strength of stabilizing factors:......

....

  Share of voice vs brand
  share: ....

....

Strength of destabilizing
factors:..............................

....

Final comments

The first comment to make in this last, short summary is a 'disclaimer'. In order to explain and elaborate on how the marketing discipline needs to move forward into the next century, one must generalize. I have deliberately simplified a number of issues in order to highlight the important aspects, and in many cases avoided an academic approach that would have included all the ifs and buts. For instance, media advertising does not always stabilize a system; there are many exceptions, but as a rule it does what is claimed in the book—i.e. builds relations that stabilize a market position.

The main purpose of this last chapter is to focus on what I see as the key issues. Each business is unique and faces a unique set of circumstances but many aspects of marketing management remain of universal importance. In our profession we are also exposed to non-repetitive repetitiveness.

To gain advantage in the future, the following will be the crucial issues:

1 Treat the unexpected as the norm. Think laterally. Remember that most, if not all, relationships are non-linear.
2 Look for probabilities rather than predictions, recognizing the non-repetitive repetitiveness. If you understand the reasons for success you will also increase the probability of success.
3 Nurture change—change is a necessity for development and commercial progress. Stability is the unwanted exception.
4 Influence and nudge the markets; look for multiplier effects to get leverage.
5 Companies, customers and competitors interact and influence each other. Neither the 'market' nor the customers are in a 'black box' but form part of a system, so expect and respect feedback.
6 Markets are aggregates of individual decision makers, in consumer as well as industrial goods and services. 'Act locally, think globally' is still relevant.

7 Be aware of how the marketing mix will affect the market system
   and use the mix to stabilize or destabilize, depending on the
   objectives. Use the leverage the economies of scale can give.
8 Always aim for being better than 'the other guy'. Attend to the
   details and build an aggregate that is superior.
9 Be fast and flexible, act on the basis of knowledge, and never
   forget the feedback loops.

Index